Postgraduate Education and Training in the Social Sciences

Processes and Products

of related interest

Graduate Education in Britain
Tony Becher, Mary Henkel and Maurice Kogan
ISBN 1 85302 531 3
Higher Education Policy Series 17

Students, Courses and Jobs
The Relationship Between Higher Education and the Labour Market
J.L. Brennan, E.S. Lyon, P.A. McGeevor and K. Murray
ISBN 1 85302 538 0
Higher Education Policy Series 21

Academic Community
Discourse or Discord?
Edited by Ronald Barnett
ISBN 1 85302 534 8
Higher Education Policy Series 20

Transition to Work
The Experiences of Former ERASMUS Students
Ulrich Teichler and Friedhelm Maiworm
ISBN 1 85302 543 7
Higher Education Policy Series 28
ERASMUS Monograph No.18

Postgraduate Education and Training in the Social Sciences
Processes and Products

Edited by Robert G. Burgess

Jessica Kingsley Publishers
London and Bristol, Pennsylvania

First published in the United Kingdom in 1994 by
Jessica Kingsley Publishers Ltd
116 Pentonville Road
London N1 9JB, England
and
1900 Frost Road, Suite 101
Bristol, PA 19007, U S A

Copyright © 1994 the contributors and the publisher

Library of Congress Cataloging in Publication Data

British Library Cataloguing in Publication Data
Burgess, Robert G.
Postgraduate Education and Training in
the Social Sciences: Processes and
Products. - (Higher Education Policy
Series)
I. Title II. Series
300.71

ISBN 1-85302-533-X

Printed and Bound in Great Britain by
Biddles Ltd, Guildford and King's Lynn

Contents

Part III: Completion and Employment

Preface

Despite widespread discussion and debate in higher education in the last ten years concerning postgraduate education and training there is relatively little research on this field of study. Indeed, where studies are available they are mainly North American in origin, or concentrated on the physical sciences and technology in the UK. Accordingly, the ESRC Training Board established a Research into Training programme to help fill this gap. This programme consisted of nine projects. One project was concerned with research students in the labour market while the others focused on the research training process. Five studies used quantitative and administrative data while the others focused on qualitative investigations.

The projects have reported separately to the ESRC and are also involved in broader dissemination through papers, articles and other materials. Accordingly, it was agreed by all the projects that contributed to this initiative that a dissemination conference would be held in Cambridge in September 1992 which would bring together some of the main findings established on this initiative where the focus was the social science PhD in the UK. The papers in this volume are concerned with the process of supervision in years one, two and three; the activities of supervisors and students; the relationships between them and their perceptions of doing a PhD. In addition, there are also papers concerned with writing, examining, completion rates and labour market studies.

All these issues are brought together in this collection in order to provide a portrait of postgraduate education and training in the social sciences. In this respect it is envisaged that the papers will be relevant for a wide audience, including supervisors and students of doctoral candidates, researchers concerned with higher education in general and postgraduate education in particular, and policy makers concerned with the future of postgraduate education.

In preparing these papers for publication I have been assisted by all members of the project teams. I would therefore like to thank my colleagues for their assistance and support. Finally I am also indebted to Su Powell, Pat Lyness and Sylvia Moore for secretarial assistance in preparing this manuscript.

Robert G. Burgess
University of Warwick

Chapter 1

Some Issues in Postgraduate Education and Training in the Social Sciences
An Introduction

Robert G. Burgess

The last decade has witnessed considerable change in the structure, content and policy associated with postgraduate education and training. Traditionally there has been a separation between policy level discussions concerning the future of postgraduate training and the practice of PhD supervision. Indeed, in many higher education institutions, postgraduate work has fitted uneasily between undergraduate education on the one hand and research on the other. In recent years, many discussions between research councils, learned societies and higher education institutions have come together to focus on a number of issues including the improvement of PhD submission and completion rates, the reduction of drop-out rates among doctoral candidates, and the provision of formal training programmes at postgraduate level.

The origin of doctoral training lies in the German and American higher education systems. Initially the PhD was introduced into Germany and adapted for North America. Subsequently, it was imported into Britain at the beginning of the twentieth century, as it was only in 1917 that the University of Oxford introduced the degree of PhD (Geiger 1985, Simpson 1983). While other universities took on doctoral candidates it was found that by 1938 there were only 3000 postgraduates in UK universities; this constituted 6 per cent of the total population. Indeed, it was only in the 1960s that considerable expansion took place, given the demands of the academic labour market consequent upon changes in the higher education system, the expansion of student numbers, the development of new universities and the establishment of polytechnics.

Trends in postgraduate research in UK universities

Statistical data on the numbers of postgraduates in the UK higher education system are difficult to obtain. Using data from the Universities Statistical Record, Burgess, Hogan, Pole and Sanders (1993) have indicated there were 45,757 postgraduate research students in UK universities in 1990/91. Of these 68,777 (63%) were full-time and 16,980 (37%) were part-time. The total number of research students increased by 9 per cent (3,730) since 1986/87. However, this did not match a 27 per cent increase in postgraduate students registered for taught courses, including master's degrees, diplomas and certificates during that period. In addition, Henkel and Kogan (1993) have reported that there were approximately 4,190 research students in public sector institutions during 1987/88, of whom 2,640 were full-time and 1,550 part-time – a significant proportion given the mission statements of institutions in the polytechnic sector to concentrate on applied rather than fundamental research. The main trends are summarised in Table 1.1.

Table 1.1: Postgraduate research students in UK universities 1986/87 to 1990/91

	1986/7 (000s)	1987/8 (000s)	1988/9 (000s)	1989/90 (000s)	1990/1 (000s)	% Change Since 1989/90
Research Students	42.0	43.0	43.9	44.3	45.7	3.2
Total Postgraduates	91.2	92.2	98.2	103.9	112.1	7.8
Research Students as % of Total Postgraduates	46.1	46.6	44.7	42.6	40.8	-1.8
Total Students	360.8	366.9	383.6	404.8	428.8	5.9
Research Students as % of Total Students	11.6	11.7	11.4	10.9	10.7	-0.2

Source: University Statistics, 1990–91, 1989–90, 1988–89, 1987–88, 1986–87, Universities Statistical Record

The number of doctorates that have been awarded in UK universities have increased by 26 per cent between 1986 and 1990 when 8,188 doctoral candidates were presented. Of those candidates who gained doctorates, 683 students were classified as social scientists: 150 in business and financial studies, 28 in librarianship and information science, 207 in education and 63 in multi-disciplinary studies. These students constitute social scientists who were engaged in postgraduate education and training in the UK.

The social science PhD

By the mid-1980s it was evident that there were problems concerned with the submission and completion of the social science PhD, given that the proportion of candidates submitting a PhD thesis in four years was only 18.2 per cent of those who began their training in 1980. As a consequence the ESRC developed an institutional sanctions policy in universities and polytechnics whereby ESRC studentships were not granted to institutions for two years if their student submission rate was under 10 per cent in 1985, 25 per cent in 1986, 35 per cent in 1987 and 40 per cent in 1988 (currently in 1993 a submission rate of 50% is required). Alongside this sanctions policy an investigation was established under the chairmanship of Graham Winfield, an industrialist, who was a member of the ESRC Council. The Winfield Report (Winfield 1987) indicated there was a lack of knowledge about postgraduate training in the social sciences. As a consequence, the Winfield task force commissioned an empirical study (Young, Fogarty and McRae 1987) and a survey by a market research company (Rubashow 1986) in addition to visits they conducted to higher education institutions. The task force also invited comments from members of the social science community on postgraduate education and training. On the basis of all these data the Winfield Enquiry was able to make a series of recommendations. First, it considered that ESRC had too many studentship schemes and suggested that these should be reduced to two schemes, one of which would have a high training component and the other focused on the generation of new knowledge – a situation that led to a debate about the training-based PhD as against the knowledge-based PhD (cf. CVCP 1988). Second, it recommended that supervision could be improved through supervisor training. Finally, it suggested that institutions should provide greater guidance for prospective students, monitor student progress, provide more facilities for graduate students, and give advice on topic choice and the timetabling of student work. As a consequence of this report the ESRC decided to reduce the number of doctoral candidates funded by the Council to 250 new studentships each year from 1988/89 (although by 1993 this had increased to 350 studentships based on improved submission rates). These awards were to be allocated through a studentship competition where student and supervisor would have to submit a joint programme of research training as the ESRC Council had adopted a training-based model for the social science PhD. This was a major departure in the UK given that the British PhD contained no coursework, unlike its American counterpart. This was the policy context in which the Research into Training Programme sponsored by the ESRC Training Board took place although the projects were intended to provide medium-term strategic research findings relevant to the policies being developed by ESRC. (For further details on the policy context, see Chapter 2 of this volume and Burgess *et al.* (1993).)

The Research into Training Programme

This research programme was established by the ESRC in 1988 to examine the contribution of social science research training to the labour market, the academic and professional community and to the careers of individuals. Secondly, it examined the research training process. Thirdly, it looked at demographic patterns, responses to ESRC policy and the patterns and processes associated with different modes of training. In the end the projects that were funded focused on two areas. First, labour market studies and, second, the research training process. The projects are summarised in Table 1.2.

Table 1.2: ESRC projects funded under the Research into Training Programme

(a) **Labour Market Studies**
IMS Richard Pearson, Ian Seccombe, Geoffrey Pike, Sara Holly and Helen Connor, Institute of Manpower Studies, University of Sussex. Doctoral Social Scientists and the Labour Market.
April 1989 to September 1990.   £58,401

(b) **The Research Training Process**
Warwick Professor Robert G Burgess, Centre for Educational Development, Appraisal and Research, University of Warwick, Research Officers Dr John Hockey and Dr Christopher Pole. Becoming a Postgraduate Student: the social organisation of postgraduate training
January 1990 to December 1991.   £56,535

Cardiff Dr K.S. Delamont and Professor P Atkinson, School of Social and Administrative Studies, University of Wales College of Cardiff, Research Officer, Dr Odette Parry. The Academic Socialisation of Doctoral Students in Social Science Disciplines.
January 1990 to December 1991.   £54,896

Bristol Professor S. Acker (now Ontario Institute for the Study of Education, Toronto, Canada) and Mr T R Hill, School of Education, University of Bristol, Research Officer, Dr E Black. Students, Supervisors and the Social Science Research Training Process.
January 1990 to December 1991.   £43,695

Nottingham Dr Michael Youngman, Department of Education, University of Nottingham. Role Expectations of Research Supervisors and Students.
April 1989 to October 1989.   £5,791

Birmingham Dr G.V. Thomas and Dr E.J. Robinson, Department of Psychology, University of Birmingham, Research Officer Mr Mark Torrance. Development of Writing Skills in Doctoral Research Students.
July 1989 to June 1991.   £34,076

Birkbeck Dr Estelle Phillips, Department of Occupational Psychology, Birkbeck College, University of London, Research Officer Dr J. Chibnall. The Concept of Quality in PhD Theses and how it is Assessed.
January 1990 to December 1991.   £34,912

Plymouth Professor David Dunkerley and Professor Jeffrey Weeks, Department of Applied Social Studies, Polytechnic South West, Research Assistants Mr Dilip Chakravarti and Mr Alan Tero. Research Degrees in the Public Sector: indicators and outcomes.
January 1990 to December 1990.   £45,416

In addition, the Training Board funded a further related project:

LSE Dr Martin Bulmer and Professor Aubrey Mckennell, London School of Economics and Political Science, Research Officer, Dr Cheryl Schonhardt-Bailey. Employers' and Researchers' Experiences of Postgraduate Training in Quantitative Methods.
October 1989 to December 1991.   £57,206

Source: Bulmer (1992)

The studies included three quantitative investigations on the labour market, on training for a career in social research, and on research degrees in public sector institutions. While the studies on the labour market and training for social research used survey data, the study on public sector research degrees engaged in secondary data analysis using CNAA data. Two other quantitative studies focused on particular departments and institutions and were concerned with supervision and the writing process. Finally, there were four qualitative studies whose work was co-ordinated by Martin Bulmer (the ESRC research co-ordinator for the programme) to ensure that there was a broad coverage of the main types of UK universities and polytechnics (at the time) by region, discipline and institutional type. Institutions were visited in all parts of the country in order for these qualitative studies to take place. The diversity of research sites reflected a range of variation in terms of institutional size, numbers of graduate students, the rating that a particular department had received in the 1989 UFC Research Selectivity Exercise, whether the institution was sanctioned by ESRC, and the mix of full-time, part-time, home and overseas postgraduate students in the social sciences. The papers that arose from these projects are presented in three sections in this volume. First, a collection of papers focusing on the process of supervision, which includes material on disciplines, departments, socialisation and student culture. Secondly, papers concerned with quality, and with training provision. Thirdly, papers concerned with completion and labour market issues. While the papers that follow have been allocated to sections on the basis of their major findings, there is no neat subdivision as some of the major issues and findings of the projects indicate.

Some major issues on postgraduate education and training

Supervision

At the heart of the PhD process is research supervision (Brown and Atkins 1988). Indeed, many commentators have signalled the importance of supervision. For example, Swinnerton-Dyer (1982) commented on the way in which students in the natural sciences had greater contact with their supervisors than those in the social sciences where it was argued that daily or weekly contact was less likely to occur. Furthermore, it was regarded that topic choice often lay with the student – a situation that could result in some difficulty in the successful progress of the PhD. Within the initiative four projects focused on supervision.

Many projects reported that supervisors had rarely attended any training courses and many had learned how to supervise by trial and error, although some departments had introduced joint supervision and one department used the CNAA model. In addition, Youngman (Chapter 5) found within his sample of supervisors only one third had more than two completed PhD supervisions, while Hill, Acker and Black (Chapter 4) found that out of sixty-two supervisors who they interviewed only nine had seen ten or more students through to completion, and twenty-four had supervised fewer than six students to completion. Meanwhile, ten supervisors had still to supervise a student through to successful completion. On the basis of developing experience in supervision coupled with external constraints such as ESRC submission rates, supervisors had tended to become more directive over time, shifting roles from project managers to critical friends (see Chapter 2). However, there was also evidence that the supervisor–student relationship was critical to successful completion, (see, for example, Chapter 4 and also Salmon 1992).

The relationship between student and supervisor also resulted in socialisation into an institution, a department and a discipline. Some of these processes were formal whereas others were informal. Indeed, Elton and Pope (1989) point to the importance of collegiality in fostering a successful context for postgraduate education. Finally, critical mass was seen as significant not only in induction but also in training (see Young *et al.* 1987, and also Chapter 2).

Training

Within the UK there has been much discussion in the social science community about training given the issue of the ESRC Guidelines during the period of the research programme (ESRC 1991). Within the research programme there was evidence of training programmes developing between formal and informal (structured and less structured) introductions to the PhD. However, Chapter 3 reports that in anthropology research training was seen as of less significance.

Among the topics in research training that were found to be valuable was the development of writing skills, a topic that is dealt with in greater depth in Chapter 6. Finally, Chapter 10 suggests that employers consider that there is (at least at the time when the study was conducted) insufficient training for social science postgraduates.

Disciplines and departments

We have already seen that the PhD was focused on academic disciplines – a situation that has been identified by other commentators (Clark 1993, Becher 1989). Indeed, Chapter 3 points to the importance of academic boundaries being clearly identified in single-discipline departments, while, even in a multi-disciplinary context, there was some evidence of disciplinary allegiance. Overall, the discipline was the focus of most students' experience and in particular was where they obtained their intellectual identity. The size of the student group within departments also has been found to be a critical factor by Young *et al.* (1987) in their study of six universities.

Nevertheless, the opportunities to study full-time are not available to all students. Indeed, Chapter 8 reports that over half of the 648 candidates successfully completing research degrees who were entered on the CNAA database studied part-time, while only 37 per cent studied full-time. The condition of part-time students has also been commented on in Chapter 4, where the concepts 'detached' and 'semi-detached' are used to refer to part-time students in Education and Psychology. The 'detached' students, who were found in Education departments, tended to have a full-time job in Education which was their main commitment, while the 'semi-detached' students more commonly found in Psychology departments tended to work as research assistants as well as for their degree courses.

Overall the evidence about critical mass is somewhat contradictory. Some studies have indicated that size is a key factor. Indeed, Chapter 2 demonstrates this, as did the study conducted by Young *et al.* (1987). However, other studies, such as Bowen and Rudenstine (1992) writing in the USA, indicate that it is the scale of the graduate programme that influences submission and completion rates, and that smaller programmes result in success. However, it is important to recall that 'small' programmes in the United States are much larger than their UK counterparts.

Quality

The concept of quality in relation to higher education has passed into common parlance in recent years (see Harvey and Green 1993). In particular, notions of quality control, quality management and academic audit have been introduced into higher education with the result that there has been concern about the way in which these ideas are handled in relation to doctoral candidates and the PhD thesis.

Within the PhD period, quality management and quality control occur at the time of admission and also in relation to monitoring student progress and upgrading, as well as in relation to the examination process. The upgrading process has been discussed in Chapter 2, while the features associated with examination are discussed in Chapter 9, which attempts to study the qualities that are looked for in PhD theses by examiners. This study focuses not only on the way in which examiners are appointed but also looks at the examination process and the extent to which it could be regarded as a *rite de passage* in the academic community.

Completion and labour market issues

The main study concerned with labour market issues came from the Institute of Manpower Studies (see Chapter 4) and focused on doctoral social scientists in the labour market. The study showed that 850 students gained doctorates in social science subjects in 1989. Their survey indicated that one third of students were from overseas, half the home students were part-time and two out of five were women. ESRC-funded students accounted for a quarter of the full-time home candidates. While the academic labour market was the main source of employment for PhD candidates the remainder were spread across a range of occupations, with small numbers being found in any one sector. Probably the most disturbing finding of all was that many employers could see no advantage in the employment of doctoral candidates, who were often considered alongside first degree students. In this respect the possession of a PhD had little value in terms of earnings (Swinnerton-Dyer 1982, Rudd 1990). Some of the findings from the IMS study were also confirmed in the study conducted by Bulmer and his colleagues (Chapter 10), who also found that employers saw no particular advantage in postgraduate qualifications at doctoral level.

Future recommendations: research and policy

The studies that are reported in this volume indicate that we have only just begun to explore some of the issues concerned with postgraduate training. As a consequence further research is needed in this area. In particular some topics for further exploration would include: the relationship between training programmes and submission and completion; changes in the training of postgraduate students, especially in the light of the ESRC Guidelines; supervision of students, especially in relation to full-time and part-time candidates; the writing process and the ways in which writing skills can be developed.

Finally, there are a number of issues concerned with policy and practice that need to be considered. First, the development of training activities for supervisors. Second, the development of teaching materials for students concerning the doctoral process. Finally, a debate needs to be stimulated among employers concerning the training that is provided at doctoral level and the opportunities to employ doctoral candidates with relevant skills in research in the social sciences. There is much work still to be done on postgraduate education through research, evaluation and policy making.

References

Becher, T. (1989) *Academic Tribes and Territories: Intellectual Inquiries and the Cultures of Disciplines*. Milton Keynes: Open University Press.

Bowen, W.G. and Rudenstine, N.L. (1992) *In Pursuit of the PhD*. Princeton, N.J.: Princeton University Press.

Brown, G. and Atkins, M. (1988) *Effective Teaching in Higher Education*. London: Methuen.

Bulmer, M. (1992) *The Research Into Training Programme: An Overview, for the ESRC Training Board* (mimeo). (Available from the author).

Burgess, R.G., Hogan, J.V., Pole, C.J. and Sanders, L. (1993) *Postgraduate Research Training in the United Kingdom*. Paris: OECD.

Clark, B.R. (1993) *The Research Foundations of Graduate Education: Germany, Britain, France, United States and Japan*. Berkeley: University of California Press.

Committee of Vice Chancellors and Principals (CVCP) (1988) *The British PhD*. London: CVCP.

Economic and Social Research Council (ESRC) (1991) *Postgraduate Training Guidelines*. Swindon: ESRC.

Elton, L. and Pope, M. (1989) Research Supervision: the value of collegiality. *Cambridge Journal of Education* 19, 3, 267–275.

Geiger, R.L. (1985) The Home of Scientists: a perspective on university research. In B. Wittrock and A. Elzinga (eds) *The University Research System: the public policies of the home of scientists*. Stockholm: Almqvist and Wicksell.

Harvey, L. and Green, D. (1993) *Quality in Higher Education*. Birmingham: BERA.

Henkel, M. and Kogan, M. (1993) Research training and graduate education: The British macrostructure. In B.R. Clark (ed) *The Research Foundations of Graduate Education: Germany, Britain, France, United States and Japan*. Berkeley: University of California Press.

Rubashow, N. (1986) *Survey of PhD Completion Rates*. London: Methuen.

Rudd, E. (1990) The early careers of social science graduates and the value of a PhD. *Journal of the Royal Statistical Society*, A 153, 2, 203–232.

Salmon, P. (1992) *Achieving a PhD*. Stoke on Trent: Trentham Books.

Simpson, R. (1983) *How the PhD Came to Britain*. Guildford: Society for Research in Higher Education.

Swinnerton Dyer, P. (1982) *Report of the Working Party on Postgraduate Education*. London: HMSO.

Winfield, G. (1987) *The Social Science PhD: The ESRC Inquiry on Submission Rates*. London: ESRC.

Young, K., Fogarty. M.P. and McRae, S. (1987) *The Management of Doctoral Studies in the Social Sciences*. London: Policy Studies Institute.

Part I

The Process of Supervision

Chapter 2

Strategies for Managing and Supervising the Social Science PhD

*Robert G. Burgess, Christopher J. Pole
and John Hockey*

Much of the policy debate concerning completion, submission and
the breadth of the PhD in the social sciences was examined in the
Winfield Report (1987). This report considered a number of models
for the education and training of PhD students. Central to the debate,
and to the Winfield enquiry, was the tension apparent in the various
definitions of what constitutes a PhD. On the one hand there was a
body of opinion that was concerned to maintain a traditional knowledge-based doctorate involving an original contribution to knowledge and embracing a process which brought students to the point
at which they could carry out research independently (Floud 1987).
On the other hand there were academics who were convinced that
the way forward for the PhD was for it to contain large elements of
formal training (Abell 1987, Wilson 1987). On occasion pronounce-
ments can be found which combine these two interrelated purposes.
A major statement came in a report published by the Committee of
Vice Chancellors and Principals (CVCP 1988). Within this document
the purpose of the PhD was summarised in the following terms:

1. The first is to enable young people of high intellectual ability
   to *develop* and bring to fruition as far as possible the quality
   of originality, to contribute new and significant ideas and to
   make a positive contribution to knowledge and creativity in
   their respective disciplines.

2. The second is to provide a training in research methods which
   makes them capable, subsequently, of assuming the role of
   independent scholars and research workers at the highest
   level, capable of planning and carrying to completion a well
   conceived plan of research directed towards a given
   objective without the necessity of supervision from
   experienced people.

The tension between these views is apparent within the literature generally. For example, Wakeford (1985) talks of the 'gentleman scholar' and 'apprenticeship models', while Young, Fogarty and McRae (1987 pp.54–55) discuss doctoral studies in terms of product or process. Furthermore, the ESRC firmly adheres to a training based PhD which has been the subject of considerable debate.

The radical nature of this policy can be appreciated in the context of comparing the British PhD with its US counterpart. While in North America there has been large amounts of coursework, in Britain the PhD has traditionally contained no coursework component. Furthermore the ESRC (and its predecesor the SSRC) had previously played a relatively minor role in postgraduate education, apart from a small experimentally funded doctoral programme where students spent the first two years of their three-year study period attending formal lectures (Silk 1988).

The latest developments from the ESRC provide a set of guidelines for the first year of postgraduate study, where institutions and supervisors are required to actively manage postgraduate education with up to 60 per cent of the first year of a PhD being devoted to coursework (ESRC 1991, p.4). This was the policy context in which debates about the management and supervision of postgraduate education occurred at the start of our project and which helped to frame some of the questions that we raised and located within a sociological context.

The research project

Our study was concerned with the process of becoming a PhD student and therefore focused on the organisation of postgraduate study, the socialisation (formal and informal) of students into postgraduate study and the relationships between students and supervisors in their first year. In this respect, our project complemented the study of second and third year PhD students conducted by Parry, Atkinson and Delamont (see Chapter 3). We focused on different disciplines and higher education institutions from those used by other teams. In particular, our project was designed to include three economics departments located within universities, three sociology departments, two of which were located in universities and one in a then polytechnic, and three business schools located in universities.

In the nine institutions we collected three kinds of data. First, documentary evidence, including prospectuses, regulations, charts, diagrams and other memoranda. Second, observational data of departments and institutions. Third, data from in-depth interviews with postgraduates, supervisors, heads of departments, deans of faculties and administrative staff concerned with graduate studies. This approach has resulted in a range of methodological issues concerning team-based research, cross-site comparison and the study of familiar settings (Hockey 1993, Pole 1993). Indeed, the familiarity of higher education institutions was the subject of considerable debate among our team as we sought to find ways to distance ourselves from our topic of study in order to pose critical questions. In these circumstances the stance of the naive researcher is inappropriate as higher education institutions were familiar to the research team, even when different from the institutions in which they studied and worked (Cottrell and Letherby 1994).

This project was located within the sociology of education with a view to extending some of the concepts that have been used in this sub-field when studying schools to the study of higher education institutions in general and postgraduate studies in particular. The approach used was symbolic interactionism (Rock 1979) which led our team to focus on certain areas and concepts including contexts, perspectives, strategies, negotiations and careers. For the purpose of this chapter we take the concept of strategy that has become regarded as central to interactionism. Strategies are a way of achieving goals through meeting internal and external constraints. In this respect, strategies for managing and supervising the social science PhD could be examined in relation to the constraints that existed outside higher education institutions and those that existed within them. It was also important to take account of the organisation of the higher education institution, the resources that were available for postgraduate study as well as the students who came forward to study in particular disciplines. Overall, the use of the term strategy allowed us to look at the aims of postgraduate study, hidden and overt, the range of strategies that were deployed institutionally and by supervisors, and the links between theory and practice.

In writing about the relationship between cultures, perspectives and strategies in relation to the socialisation of student teachers, Lacey remarks:

> As a group of individuals develop or acquire a sense of common purpose, so the sets of strategies adopted by them acquire a common element. It is this common element that enables the common perspective to emerge. As the perspective develops and if over a long period of time, the situations that continually face the group have a common element, then the understandings broaden and develop to produce a sub-culture. The mark of the sub-culture is that its most important elements are not immediately lost if the individual leaves the group and the common

situation of the group members. Perspectives are more quickly taken up and dropped than sub-cultures. To be sure the elements of sub-culture are often suppressed and can be almost completely covered by later behaviour patterns, but the supposition here is that these elements affect changes deep within the personality structure of the individual and are responsible for the richness, complexity and uniqueness of individual personality.

(Lacey 1977 p.70)

Within our study we were interested in the common elements involved in the strategies used, not only by individual supervisors but also by other members of the institutions in which they were located. In this respect, we were interested in examining strategies that were used to manage the PhD organisationally as well as individually in the student–supervisor relationship. Indeed, individuals supervise in the context of institutional or departmental requirements and all these issues needed to be explored. Accordingly, we were interested in such questions as: what strategies are adopted by higher education institutions? How do supervisors define and organise the conduct of the PhD in the first year of study?

The organisation of the PhD

In order to define organisation in the context of doctoral studies, it is important to consider the extent to which an identifiable programme existed for first year PhD students. Second, the administrative arrangements for the PhD, including the existence of a postgraduate Board of Study and the effects of its impact upon students, were also examined. Finally, the organisation of supervision in terms of single or joint supervision and other administrative or advisory bodies with whom the student may have contact require some consideration. In this context, organisation refers to structures put in place by the members of higher education institutions in order to facilitate the effective management of PhD students both intellectually and administratively (cf. Young *et al.* 1987).

The PhD programme

In terms of an identifiable PhD programme it is possible to construct two models of organisation. On the one hand there is the highly structured programme which requires students to follow specific courses in research methods and in their substantive area. Such a model also includes a requirement for students to produce work for assessment or to sit examinations. Under such arrangements the first year operates as a qualifying period during which students gain the necessary knowledge and skills to embark on their PhD which would not effectively begin until the second year (although a small proportion of time would be devoted to the thesis topic). During this qualifying year students would usually be registered for the degree of M.Phil with transfer to PhD occurring only after satisfactory completion of the first year.

At the other end of the spectrum is the unstructured or loosely structured model which places no requirement on students to attend courses or produce pieces of work which are not directly related to their own research projects. This model of PhD organisation, which was termed the traditional approach, assumes that students receive the required support and guidance from their supervisors or are able to acquire it independently. Students in this situation may also be registered initially for an M.Phil degree. However, their upgrading would not be dependent on completion of examinations or particular courses but upon satisfactory progress during the first year. Satisfactory progress was judged by supervisors and by the production of progress reports for supervisors and funding bodies. Such a model assumes no qualitative difference between the first and subsequent years in terms of the ultimate aim of the research as, despite students being registered for an M.Phil, their aim is a PhD. In this sense, the first year is not a qualifying year but is perceived by students as an integral part of the PhD.

Among the nine research sites it is possible to identify PhD programmes at either end of the highly structured–unstructured continuum and at various points between. For example, the most highly structured programme required students to follow courses in research methods, social statistics and epistemology, to complete a literature review, write essays and make a presentation of their research intentions based on their first year work before being upgraded from M.Phil to PhD. In another context, such courses were intended to provide basic familiarity with research methods, appropriate theoretical approaches, statistical techniques and to develop analytic and writing skills. Alternatively, or in addition, courses were also used for students to experiment with research design, to pilot research instruments and to develop and refine research proposals. Yet, at the same time, the first year was also important for the socialisation of students into a particular academic or disciplinary or institutional culture. Indeed, some courses were seen to have a social as well as an intellectual purpose. Overall, the highly structured first year was seen not only as a transition period from undergraduate to postgraduate work but also as a preparatory strategy to equip students to conduct their research successfully from a position of confi-

dence. In economics numerous supervisors described it as an opportunity for students to 'tool up' on research techniques in order to
conduct their research in the following two years. As one supervisor
explained:

> I think the only way you can justify it [the PhD] is in terms of
> building up a methodological foundation for the researcher to do
> research in the future. You have to start from the position that
> there is a lot of methodology to be learnt, partly in a formal way
> and partly by using it. Until such time as they've learnt this
> methodology, they won't be proper researchers.

At the same time, the rationale for compulsory courses in epistemology was offered in terms of an opportunity to provide students with
broader intellectual development which would help them to locate
their research problem intellectually before starting to collect and
analyse data. An important corollary of this strategy is that many
departments hoped that the benefit of the structured or taught first
year programme would be realised in terms of submission and
completion rates for the departments concerned.

Where less structured programmes were offered there was a
greater emphasis on the individual to equip him or herself with the
necessary tools and knowledge to conduct research. Opportunities
to follow courses and attend seminars existed, but although students
may have been encouraged to attend there was no compulsion. In
one institution, first year PhD students could join taught MA courses
which were relevant to their research. Here they were invited to
attend and to present research seminars, as well as going to courses
provided centrally by the university on computing, word processing
and writing styles. In another institution, a summer school for PhD
students was held each year, during which these and other topics
were discussed. All first year students were required to attend the
summer school.

Within the project, some disciplinary differences in the provision
of a structured doctoral programme during the first year were revealed. For example, the most highly structured programmes were
offered in business schools and economics departments, whilst the
sociology departments tended to offer loosely structured or unstructured programmes. However, more significant was the number of
first year students registered in the department. Those institutions
offering structured first year programmes had relatively large numbers of students (12–20 in our study) whilst those providing only a
loosely structured programme tended to have only a small number
of students. In those cases where a structured programme was offered, the approach to the PhD and the definition applied to it by staff

emphasised its importance as a means of research training. The emphasis tended to be less on independent isolated scholarship (see Delamont and Eggleston 1983) and more on the PhD as an apprenticeship in research and academia. One business school professor described PhD students as 'journeymen' (cf. Rouse 1984) explaining that once they had achieved their 'ticket' they could move freely within the subject. Within those institutions offering a more traditional approach to the PhD, emphasis was placed on individual scholarship and on the substantive area of study rather than on the acquisition of research skills. In this context, research skills and academic socialisation were a means to an end rather than an end in themselves.

Administrative arrangements

Just as the arrangements for research training could be placed on a structured to unstructured continuum so the same applied to the way in which administrative activities were conducted in respect of monitoring student progress and upgrading students from the degree of M.Phil to PhD. In all institutions these administrative arrangements were the responsibility of a postgraduate Board of Study, a Doctoral Research Board, a Higher Degrees Committee or its equivalent. In addition to co-ordinating the work of departments or faculty boards, these structures took on various institution-wide responsibilities. However, the strategies that were deployed by members of these bodies depended upon the context in which they were located. For example, some operated as a mechanism for monitoring progress, ensuring students were on-line for submission by a required date, arbitrated in disputes between students and supervisors, and reviewed the position of graduate students with regard to resources. One Sub-Dean for research indicated the way in which he had established a formal structure. He explained that when he took on his role:

> There was a wide variety of approaches to the business of conducting the annual monitoring exercise, monitoring of progress and also a wide variety of approaches in approaching the upgrading decision and I felt as though there were certain principles which in some way ought to be adhered to but which in some instances were probably not being followed. For instance I felt it was important that the responsibilities for supervision should be separated from the responsibilities for monitoring progress that it should not be one and the same person who is both supervising the student and then monitoring their progress on an annual basis. So in my capacity as Sub-Dean I drew up a kind of statement

of good practice in monitoring progress which was a series of points suggesting that, for instance, supervision should be separated from monitoring, that departments should appoint a departmental postgraduate tutor who would chair a departmental postgraduate committee that would be responsible for the monitoring of progress, that monitoring should be conducted on the basis of formal submissions – the contents of which were related to the year of study of the candidate. There was a list of 14 or 15 points. Now that particular statement of good practice was endorsed by faculty and commended to departments but faculty has no power.

In this instance, the faculty had devised a framework within which monitoring would take place. It was this strategy which was linked to the management of PhD work on the one hand and to supervision on the other. Monitoring was also a faculty responsibility in another institution where a Sub-Dean for research explained the system, which in this instance was more informal:

> There's certainly a system whereby progress reports are submitted by the supervisors to the faculty so I suppose you could say that was the monitoring system. I could think of a case where the supervisor has suggested that progress was other than satisfactory and the faculty business committee then oversaw some remedial programme to bring the student up to scratch. One of the difficulties, I think, in this area is that there's not sufficient uniformity of perception amongst supervisors as to what these procedures actually mean and so a supervisor who is a very hard task master or mistress may make some slightly critical comments which are then given more attention than they perhaps deserve whereas your average supervisor might just say satisfactory progress and have a quiet word with the student. So again there's an element of educating people to the system I think still to be done.

However, in this instance the actual review of student progress was conducted by the faculty secretary who, it was argued, had the most continuity of experience in this area, as the Sub-Dean explained:

> Deans and Vice-Deans come and go and the members of the business committee the same, although I think to be honest I've relied very heavily on certain rather willing people to fill these positions. But it is the faculty secretary that provides the most continuity and I think in a sense if the supervisor's reports say no problems then there's not very much more to be done.

In this institution it was the faculty secretary who scrutinised individual progress reports and brought them to the attention of a formal committee.

In contrast, in another institution the way in which the organisation dealt with student monitoring was outside departments but the decision-making power on student progress lay with the Sub-Dean for postgraduate research. He explained this in the following terms:

Now in the progress reports that have to be made on students... you will see that there is a question there at the end of the first year. It basically asks them how far they have fulfilled the programme of work they'd agreed with their supervisor and whether they have agreed a programme for the coming year. So you can see how it won't be all that difficult to move in on other departments and say 'well you know you say you're fulfilling your first year's programme but you're agreeing a second year programme of work, let us now agree a first year and make that part of the actual application' because among other things we want to make sure the supervisor knows what they're doing. They've got to be a party to that negotiation so I think that's a fairly easy step. Now this year, for example, a couple of people came in and said they had not filled in the section on how far they had fulfilled last year's work programme. I sent it back and that student could not be registered for the new year until that was filled in. Another one came in from a part-time student with no work programme agreed for the coming year. I sent that back and said you've got to have a programme for the coming year and I think the supervisor said something about 'well he's a very awkward customer as you can see from his report'. I said 'I don't care, you've got to have a programme for the coming year' so what I want to do, as you can see, is to move that process back to make it part of the admissions process, because we're damn well not going to fall short of the ESRC completion or whoever finances them. Whatever the completion period is we are going to conform to that.

In these cases, supervisors would need to take account of strategies being deployed within the universities concerned. In one, a very formal structure based on a committee, in another responsibility effectively lay with the supervisor, while in a third responsibility lay with an individual who held the post of Sub-Dean for postgraduates. In addition, the strategies that were deployed were not only the result of internal constraints but also external constraints, as several institutions mentioned the influence of the ESRC's submission rate policy.

Similarly, upgrading took a similar form to monitoring where examples could be located on a formal to informal continuum. In all departments, students were registered for an MPhil degree for a period of time before being upgraded to PhD. The process by which upgrading took place varied between institutions and could involve the submission of written work reflecting progress made during a specified time. In turn it could be accompanied by the requirement for students to defend their work before an upgrading committee, and one institution required students to pass written examinations. The strategy in this case was designed to ensure that students made sufficient progress to warrant upgrading and had the ability to cope with doctoral work. The strategy was intended to facilitate a fit between the type of student in terms of ability and commitment, and the demands of the degree for which he or she was registered. In common with the structured taught first year, the upgrading procedures were designed to screen out those students who, for whatever reason, looked unlikely to succeed at doctoral level, and thereby ensure a positive submission rate and successful completion rate. In one institution the opinion of one senior member of staff was that the upgrading and review strategy was a means of ensuring that the department was not carrying any passengers. As he stated:

If they are no good after the first year they can bugger off.

In other institutions such a hard and fast approach did not exist and strategies were put in place to support the students through the first year. For example, in several institutions Graduate Review Boards were in place to which students reported periodically. Such strategies not only checked on student progress but also on the student–supervisor relationship. The most formal procedures involved in upgrading students existed in the polytechnic which was following the CNAA regulations. Here an Assistant Director explained the upgrading procedure in the following terms:

For all research degree students there is a very close monitoring process. I mean in particular it's particularly focused at the MPhil/PhD transfer level, where they have to go through not only preparation of a report but an oral with an internal person chairing and an external person also independent of the course who comes in that subject area, who will evaluate that project so that that's a very careful scrutiny. Now that's been in existence for a very long time but more focused. It used to be voluntary but now it's compulsory, you have to go through that process, so we've tightened up on that and then again that being introduced about the end of 1991. So you can see a rapid change in the institution over the three years since independence. Most of the ideas were floating around but they just hadn't gelled.

In this instance the strategy deployed for the upgrading was the result of external constraints imposed through the CNAA regulations which continued to be used when the institution gained independent status. In contrast, universities involved in this study indicated a less formal structure. However some did have a structure within which the upgrading process was located. As one Sub-Dean explained:

> The recommendation comes from the department to faculty. Now each department will approach that task in very different ways. Some will have much more systematic departmental procedures than others for determining the basis upon which that recommendation should be made. In some instances departments will insist, for instance, that the person has completed a full research proposal with a detailed research timetable, has got a fully specified design methodology sorted out and a recommendation will only be forwarded on the basis of that sort of evidence. In other cases I think it's done on a much more relaxed and casual basis.

In this instance, the Faculty had taken an innovative role and put in place a framework within which upgrading should occur. This procedure owed much to the ESRC policy of recognising institutions for postgraduate study, the review mechanisms required for postgraduate studentship holders and the ESRC sanctions policy.

Meanwhile, in other institutions a more informal approach was still in existence, as a Sub-Dean explained:

> I think we have probably a number of systems now for the way in which people are registered. The normal pattern is that they're registered for an MPhil and then they're upgraded at some appropriate moment and I think that's usually at the insistence of the department and the detailed work will be done there. And, indeed, in this department we resolved a little while ago that it would be done by a collective meeting of supervisors, that all the cases would be considered collectively, although I'm not sure that we've got to the stage of first implementing that system.

This system was without formality at departmental level as decisions were effectively being taken by individual supervisors. Nevertheless, these decisions had to be processed through the committee structure of the university. However, as administrators in this institution and elsewhere indicated, if departments made positive recommendations it was unlikely that they would be overturned elsewhere within the system. Across all disciplines, upgrading of all students from MPhil to PhD was the formal responsibility of administrative boards or committees who acted as gatekeepers and appeared to have considerable power over students. This was the case where formal meetings occurred, but in other instances it was the responsibility of student and supervisor. Nevertheless, failure to be upgraded was a fear that virtually all students discussed. In particular, for overseas students, many of whom were university teachers in their own countries, it could prove disastrous as a failure to be upgraded could result in the loss of financial support from their governments and the loss of their job or a block to promotion.

The organisation of supervision

Apart from the polytechnic, where supervisory organisation was governed by CNAA regulations, the majority of students were supervised by one member of staff. In a minority of cases students were jointly supervised by two staff. Where joint supervision existed it was often to combine the expertise of supervisors in order to cover more adequately the student's research topic. Alternatively where a member of staff was inexperienced in supervision he or she would be supported by a more experienced colleague. Several experienced supervisors drew a distinction between relevant disciplinary knowledge and craft knowledge. Our data suggest a trend in which the more experienced a supervisor is, the more likely he or she is prepared to supervise a student in an area outside his or her specialism. One experienced supervisor explained:

> When I was a very young supervisor I'd supervise in areas which I felt expert in. I think I'm now prepared to admit my inadequacies and failings in the literature etc. and to take people on in something broader, taking slightly more risks on the subject area and saying 'I think I've learnt a few tricks as far as supervision is concerned'.

Where such an approach is taken by supervisors the emphasis would seem to be placed on their confidence in their own ability to use a range of tactics successfully in order to ensure a positive outcome. In this situation craft knowledge takes precedence over discipline based knowledge and may be used in joint supervision where the junior member of staff has the expert disciplinary knowledge and the senior, more experienced supervisor, the craft knowledge.

Where joint supervision existed students tended to identify one person as their main supervisor and the other as a support supervisor. This seemed not to reflect the degree of contact the student had with that person but their seniority in the department, their knowledge of the research topic and their experience of supervision. Joint supervision did not ensure that students received more support or better guidance. For instance one joint supervisee recounted situations where her supervisors had disagreed over the direction of the study, its focus and the appropriate literature to pursue. The result was confusion for the student who was more concerned with producing work which would be acceptable to both supervisors than with the direction of her project and her research interests.

In addition to supervisors, students claimed to have contact with other staff in the department or, in some cases, elsewhere in the higher education institution. Such contacts were usually for specific kinds of instruction, for example obtaining information on the literature, or establishing fieldwork contacts or for particular skills in computing or statistical methods. In this respect, students had recourse to support on an informal basis which went beyond their supervisors. As one supervisor explained:

> There appears to be a kind of PhD research culture here. Students help one another, there's very much a feeling of, if someone's got a problem... For example I've got a student who's coming to see me this afternoon. She undoubtedly requires some help as far as inputting her data onto the computer is concerned, well she's getting some help from the SPSS... But she was saying, if I'm sitting in my office and I have a problem or if I'm sitting in front of a terminal here and I have a problem and there's no member of staff around then she named about four or five people, doctoral students, who said they would gladly give her some help. So there's very much a sense of let's help each other and let's make sure now that we're going to complete within four years. There's very much a completion ethos here so students know that students in the past have completed in four years and therefore they believe it can be done. Whereas I suppose in other places where you've got poor completion rates they look ahead and think well the norm here is 20 per cent completion, whereas the norm here is more or less everybody completes.

In this context, support was identified as fundamental to the start of the research process where students were introduced to a research culture and to a culture of postgraduate support and completion.

Strategies for the organisation of PhD work, the existence of a programme, and the administrative and supervisory arrangements for doctoral work are central to the experience of the first year. It is these three elements that are important for socialisation and supervision. But within the institutions in our study, the arrangements for supervision occur at departmental level where supervisors are responsible for defining their relationships with students and the strategies they will deploy.

Supervisory strategies

Strategies and tactics of supervision varied widely among those who were interviewed. Our initial data analysis did not reveal any particular pattern in relation to the disciplines studied during the first year of registration. But some similarities in style may be identified according to the supervisor's experience. None of the supervisors who were interviewed received any formal training for their role and their approach to supervision seemed to be contingent on a number of factors. These included the assessment of the student's intellectual capacities usually formed during the early stages of the supervisory relationship, their own experience as a PhD student, either attempting to replicate this or to take a totally different approach, the student's technical or research expertise and the stage of the project. However, each student brought different demands which necessitated flexibility on the part of the supervisor in terms of approach and the way in which supervision was organised.

Flexibility

Our data suggest that it is not appropriate to talk about supervisory style in the sense that the term would label a particular individual as always supervising in a particular way. The data suggest that most supervisors adopt a degree of flexibility in their approach to supervision in an attempt to meet the needs of individual students. In this sense supervisory tactics were appropriate, as one supervisor explained:

> I tend to be fairly flexible. It all depends on the student. Clearly if the student is someone who's older and knows what they're about then you can say you go and give them independence.

The tactics adopted seemed to be influenced by a range of factors. In particular, the stage of the research seemed influential, as did the supervisor's assessment of the student as a researcher. In several cases these two issues came together, the further into the PhD the student was, the greater the expectation of competence from the supervisor. This was reflected in the degree of contact between supervisor and student, as one very experienced supervisor explained:

> I see it as a meeting of at least once a week, sometimes more, of between one and three hours for maybe up to a year.

Whilst not all supervisors could be quite so generous with their time, the tactic of spending more time with students during the first year seemed common, as another supervisor explained:

> Initially we'd have regular meetings and then when she was getting on well...we used to meet once a week when she'd finished a section and then we'd develop, have a look at that and then go on to the next section, rather than saying you must come in every week.

Supervisors spoke in terms of different phases of the research programme which required different tactics and different amounts of
contact with students. Typically, fieldwork phases were times when
contact was reduced. In some cases the geographical location of the
fieldwork precluded any contact for its duration. The same supervisor continued:

> But sometime during the first summer or thereabouts... there will
> be a period of research evolving and they may start on some
> fieldwork. There are some phases of fieldwork when they are so
> busy interviewing they don't want to see me for a couple of weeks
> or not more than once a week anyway, or more briefly once a week
> for half an hour rather than three.

In this particular case the research process seemed to be divided up
into its constituent activities, and supervisory tactics relating to
contact and input from the supervisor varied accordingly. For example, the supervisor also identified analysis and thinking through
results as a time when regular and sustained contact was required,
whereas writing was seen as a solo activity, at least in terms of
producing the first draft.

Driving projects

Students saw supervisors as important to the progress of the research.
They looked towards supervisors for direction and guidance with the
literature which would underpin their projects, for assistance in
designing their research, identifying an appropriate methodology
and limiting and focusing the project. In those institutions where an
unstructured or loosely structured first year existed the supervisor
was a project manager. For example, the revision of initial research
proposals and requests for progress reports served to demonstrate to
students that there was a degree of shared responsibility for the
project. In this context, students expected to have regular and frequent contact with their supervisors. Where this did not occur students expressed concern and uncertainty about the direction of their
projects, with students suggesting that there was a sense of aimless-
ness or vagueness about where the research was heading or what it
was about (Delamont and Eggleston 1983). In these circumstances, it
became important for the supervisor, as project manager, to drive the
project in order to get the student through the PhD, as the following
comment illustrates:

> Most of the PhD students aren't that bright you know. They're
> bright enough to go through and get the degree but they're
> typically people who need a lot of hands-on attention and if the
> student appears to be of that sort and I tend to be... telling him

what to do, fix up for new appointments to see me... get them to prepare drafts of their work... push them.

Whilst for this supervisor it was usually his tactic to drive the research by setting agendas and deadlines, many students were encouraged to drive the process, by providing ideas and showing initiative, only seeking out their supervisors when necessary. An experienced supervisor explained such tactics in the following terms:

Supervisor: My door is open and certainly when they've got
              any interesting findings come and see me,
              anything interesting I want to know about it,
              anything which is any major problem come and
              talk to me about it.

CP: So you've put the emphasis, certainly after the initial
              stages, on them to drive the relationship?

Supervisor: Yes, I have to say that my nature is not to be
              particularly disciplined in doing the things
              perhaps I ought to do. For example, I don't have
              regular meetings, we don't get our diaries out and
              have the date of the next meeting in a formal
              sense ever produced.

Although the supervisor gave the impression of placing the responsibility for the supervisory relationship with the student, he went on to explain that such a relationship could only be successful where the student was committed and working hard. Where this did not occur then different tactics would be adopted, as he explained:

If a student was actually failing to some extent and if I felt this person isn't working hard enough then I'd simply have to adapt. But unlike say MBA dissertations or projects where you feel you've got to take a hard line I think here it's encourage them to feel that they can talk to me.

Clearly this supervisor has different tactics for different kinds of students and although he claims to encourage students to be autonomous and to drive the relationship, it would seem that this is in fact limited autonomy, dependent upon his assessment of student progress and the need for support.

Critical 'friends'?

As the research progressed, and students felt more confident about the direction and scope of their work, expectations of the supervisor changed. He or she was no longer the project manager but became a critical friend with whom students would have regular contact but with less frequency. Students expected to be able to call upon their supervisors for advice and guidance but as they approached the end of the first year there was a sense in which they were taking greater responsibility for their own work. Expectations changed from supervisors shaping and directing the project to pragmatic concerns such as providing fieldwork contacts, advice with software, statistical techniques and issues concerning analysis and writing.

Supervisors, whilst wishing to encourage and nurture their students, also alluded to a period during which students were required to demonstrate their capacity to cope with the PhD and to prove their intellectual worth. In one case this was achieved through the supervisor being highly critical of the student in the early stages. He explained:

> The first six months is crucial and I tend to take a very negative approach, almost discouraging them I suppose. I would keep on challenging them, as I say, critically in quite a negative way as much as I feel I can, whilst not wanting to de-motivate them, until such a time as they've demonstrated to me that they've got something which makes sense, they've got something which is really worth pursuing. At which point it's wholehearted support and then the element of you're in charge of this piece of research, I'm here as your mentor and helper.

Almost as a rite of passage the supervisor employs the tactic of requiring students to prove themselves early on (Renouff 1989). In one instance a supervisor indicated that his tactic was to be rude to students and to be critical of them. Indeed, those students who survived this process were then invited to meetings of a specialist research group that the supervisor organised. Students themselves saw this as being something to which they could aspire and through which they could prove themselves in the eyes of the supervisor. In these instances, time, together with the need to produce research ideas and plans, is used tactically to give the supervisor confidence that the student has the ability to complete the work and gain a PhD. But supervisors were also involved in establishing relationships with their students.

Academic and personal relationships

Some supervisors were concerned not only for the academic well-being of their students but also with pastoral issues. While structures did exist to help students cope with personal problems, some supervisors also considered it important to take a role in this aspect of a student's work and life. One supervisor explained:

> Also I am needed to help personally with the personal flounderings and senses of disorientation or stagnation that a person goes

through. So she [the student] and I are going to walk up a local hill on Saturday morning because she needs some encouragement.

For this supervisor the student–supervisor role involved more than academic concerns. His tactics involved ways of providing general support for the student and providing encouragement outside the academic relationship. His tactic was to combine personal with academic support.

This was often the case when supervisors were involved with overseas students, whom they considered to be in need of support with a variety of matters relating to accommodation, finance, family life and so on. One of the few women supervisors who was interviewed explained her role in this context:

> ...because they're overseas students and particularly female Muslim students don't really have much contact with other people and therefore it's always through the supervisor that they sort of seek advice and things. It's like what do I do about these poll tax forms, who do I go and see?

One of the results of this particular relationship was that student and supervisor had a fairly close academic and personal relationship which was shared by their families. She continued:

> She and her husband and her two kids come to our house and we go to their house and so you know exactly what's going on.

This close relationship enabled the supervisor to put her supervisory tactics in the context of a range of other factors relevant to the student's life. In this case the strategy for successful completion of the PhD involved tactics not just of academic guidance but of practical and pastoral support.

Rescuing and salvaging

In some cases supervisors indicated they needed to move beyond a situation where advice and guidance were given to actual input of their own. Several supervisors indicated that they felt a need to get students through the PhD particularly where students had conceptual and linguistic problems. This meant that supervisory tactics sometimes involved re-drafting theses, pulling ideas together, identifying ways of producing sufficient quality to satisfy an external examiner. Indeed, some supervisors indicated that they were cast in the role of rescuer, or, as one supervisor indicated, 'salvage expert'. One experienced supervisor explained how he rescued candidates and theses which ran into difficulties. He recalled:

I took it [the thesis] over and said look there are certain simple things you can do. You've done a lot of number crunching here – you've got a fancy programme. I said the first thing I would have done is to set up some tables and see if you could do some tests. I had him doing it all again and meanwhile I found an external and explained the situation to him, got my knuckles rapped by the Faculty for this for doing it so quickly, but this bloke said 'I'll see him next Monday' and so we went and had what was, in effect, a viva for three and a half hours or so.

In recounting the events which effectively ensured the candidate left with a PhD, the supervisor was questioning his own role and the extent to which he could use direct intervention to ensure the candidate was successful. He justified the use of these tactics in the following way:

I felt, well we have an obligation to these people. They've been here for three years and paid £12,000. If they go back without a PhD they'll probably get some part of their anatomy chopped off. You know they'll certainly lose their job.

Apart from the ethical issues involved, the supervisor raised the important issue of the need to know what is required of the candidate to be successful – a situation which resulted in students in apprenticeship to their supervisors.

Apprenticeships and partnerships

Several supervisors characterised the supervisor–student role in terms of an apprenticeship. In this respect, they saw themselves as guides or mentors who had been through the process and were now sufficiently experienced to take others through it. As one supervisor explained:

To help them through I could be seen as the master – you know the one who's gone before. I went through my apprenticeship ten years prior to that and now I'm helping other people through that very same process. Apprenticeship in coming to terms with research methodology, getting to grips with the literature, identifying a project, designing a particular piece of research, conducting it, the whole shot, and at the end of it then saying 'well you've started, now let's move on to ensure that this can be fruitfully published in a variety of ways.'

The notion of master and apprentice embraces not just supervisory practice but the ethos of partnership in which student and supervisor are jointly involved. Indeed, it suggests that partnership does not end with the successful completion of the thesis but continues to publication and into academic life.

The expectations and assumptions that students and supervisors hold of each other in terms of role, guide, project manager, critical 'friend', structured the supervisor–student relationship and the strategy that was deployed.

Conclusion

This chapter has focused on the strategies utilised to organise, administer and supervise the first year of a PhD in the social sciences. The key question is how supervisors relate to different strategies and how different strategies can be utilised in relation to the same situation. Much depends upon the supervisor's assessment of the student, their personal knowledge of students, the identification of requirements within the institution and beyond it, their views about the ways in which future supervision is to be conducted and their view of what constitutes a PhD. The strategies that are deployed by supervisors and by members of higher education institutions are designed to achieve a PhD for the student and a successful submission for the purposes of ESRC recognition although this was not always of paramount importance. Such supervision is a complex process involving a range of strategies which exist in order to meet internal and external constraints in the supervisory process.

Acknowledgement

This project entitled *Becoming a Postgraduate Student* was directed by Professor R.G. Burgess at CEDAR, University of Warwick. It was an ESRC funded project (Grant No: T00740 1011). This chapter is based on the research and the views which it represents are those of the authors. The paper does not represent ESRC policy.

References

Abell, P. (1987) PhD completion rates: some observations for the ESRC. In *The ESRC Inquiry on Submission Rates. The Background Papers.* London: ESRC.

Cottrell, P. and Letherby, G. (1994) The 'person' in the researcher. In R.G. Burgess (ed) *Issues in Qualitative Research.* London: JAI Press.

CVCP (1988) *The British PhD.* London. CVCP.

Delamont, S. and Eggleston, J. (1983) A necessary isolation?. In J. Eggleston and S. Delamont (eds) *Supervision of Students for Research Degrees.* Birmingham: BERA.

ESRC (1991) *Postgraduate Training Guidelines.* Swindon: ESRC.

Floud, R. (1987) Reflections on the PhD. In *The Social Science PhD. The ESRC Inquiry on Submission Rates. The Background Papers.* London: ESRC.

Hockey, J. (1993) Research Methods – Researching Peers and Familiar Settings. *Research Papers in Education, 8,* 2, 199–225.

Lacey, C. (1977) *The Socialisation of Teachers.* London: Methuen.

Pole, C.J. (1993) Watching Us Watching You: Sociologists Researching Social Scientists, Researching the Familiar?. Paper Presented at British Sociological Association Annual Conference, April 5–8, University of Essex.

Renouff, J. (1989) An Alternative PhD. *Area* 21, 129–130.

Rock, P. (1979) *The Making of Symbolic Interactionism.* London: Macmillan.

Rouse, L.P. (1984) Breaking into academe. *Academe.* May/June.

Silk, J. (1988) Private affluence and public austerity: motors for innovation in postgraduate training? *Journal of Geography in Higher Education 12.*

Wakeford, J. (1985) *A Sociological Study of Part-Time Postgraduate Students in Sociology and Social Administration.* London: ESRC.

Wilson, A. (1987) Research degrees and submission rates. In *The Social Science PhD. The ESRC Inquiry on Submission Rates. The Background Papers.* London: ESRC.

Winfield, G. (1987) *The Social Science PhD. The ESRC Enquiry on Submission Rates. The Report.* London: ESRC.

Young, K., Fogarty, M.P. and McRae, S. (1987) *The Management of Doctoral Studies in the Social Sciences.* London: PSI.

Chapter 3

Disciplinary Identities and Doctoral Work

*Odette Parry, Paul Atkinson
and Sara Delamont*

This chapter examines how academic work is conceptualised and carried out in different academic disciplines through the accounts given by PhD students and supervisors of doctoral work in social anthropology, development studies, urban studies and town planning.[1]

While recognising the complexity of institutional and disciplinary arrangements which inform the definition, production and reproduction of expert knowledge, we shall concentrate on two organising principles. These principles were crucial to our understanding of disciplinary work in the different sites which we visited. The first is the way in which our informants related to, or identified with, particular bodies of disciplinary knowledge. The second is the way in which this identification with particular bodies of disciplinary knowledge informed definitions of what constituted appropriate disciplinary work in each of the disciplines or departments which we visited.

The theoretical perspective with which our study most readily identifies is symbolic interactionism in that we reject a stable and unchanging view of the social world in favour of a world which takes

---

1   The data on social anthropology, development studies, urban studies and town planning in this paper were collected as part of a wider study which focused on these four disciplines plus human geography and area studies. The research examined the way in which PhD students and supervisors define and interpret the process of research, the processes of transmission of technical skills and indeterminate knowledge, the relationship between social contexts and intellectual development within disciplines/departments and the comparison of the socialisation of different types of PhD students, in contrasting institutions, in selected areas of study.

its meaning from the interpretation and interactional flow of social action. In this respect we have been particularly influenced by ideas emanating from and developed by followers of the Chicago School tradition. While recognising that 'academic socialisation' of postgraduate students does not correspond perfectly with the empirical content of much of that literature, we identify with studies of occupational socialisation carried out by Becker, Geer, Hughes and Strauss (1961), Bloom (1973), Shuval (1975) and Haas and Shaffir (1977, 1987). These studies concentrated upon how students 'made out' at school and emphasised 'situated learning' and collective coping or survival strategies.

While identifying with the theoretical and methodological assumptions of these studies[2] the present research has sought to combine this approach with our interest in the broadly structuralist perspective on academic and educational knowledge deriving in part from the work of Basil Bernstein (e.g. Bernstein 1977, 1990, and Atkinson 1985, 1991) and Pierre Bourdieu (e.g. Bourdieu 1988, Bourdieu and Passeron 1977, Robbins 1991). From this perspective we are interested in how expert knowledge is defined, produced and reproduced in sites of academic socialisation and our interests are foreshadowed by some of our previous publications in this area (Atkinson 1983, Atkinson and Delamont 1985, Parry 1991).

The organisation of academic work

Organisationally, academic work can be described in terms of subject areas, disciplines, faculties and departments. These descriptions are not however mutually exclusive. They often overlap, and arrangements vary from the very simple to the extremely complex.

The four disciplines described in this chapter were subject to different arrangements. Although all four were departments located in faculties of social science, faculty arrangements were characterised by the strength of boundary which defined each respective discipline within the faculty. Where boundaries were strongly defined then disciplines could be described as discrete or separate from each other. Where boundaries were weak, as in multi-disciplinary faculty arrangements, disciplines were less insulated and their boundaries

---

2   The research was accomplished by detailed case studies of PhD socialisation. Data were collected primarily by intensive interviews with students, supervisors and other key informants (e.g. graduate tutors, Deans).

permeable. Under these arrangements there was interflow between the different contents of disciplines within the faculty.

Disciplines themselves could also be described as either single or multi-disciplinary. In the case of the four disciplines described in this paper, anthropology was the only single discipline whereas development studies, urban studies and town planning were all multi-disciplinary in that they were made up of a number of different subject areas. For purposes of clarity we refer, in this chapter, to single disciplines as primary disciplines and multi-disciplines as secondary disciplines.

The complexity of these arrangements is well illustrated by the example of anthropology, which can be both a subject area and a primary discipline or department. Although we looked at a number of anthropology departments we also found anthropology as a subject area within the development studies disciplines.

Generally the departments and subject areas described in this chapter represent a broad spectrum of the different disciplinary arrangements described above.

Disciplinary identity

The reproduction of scholarly knowledge at the level of postgraduate research is closely linked to the reproduction or transformation of social identities. The process of postgraduate research may be described as a protracted status passage or set of status passages through which students develop.

This process involves 'situated learning' whereby students 'learn the ropes' as research students, and which has been adequately demonstrated in the 'classic' studies on occupational socialisation in regard to several different professional and occupational groups. However, we are equally interested in the fact that the process of postgraduate research also involves the acquisition of academic identity, realised through identification with intellectual traditions and groupings, with departments or disciplines, academic peer groups, networks and learned societies.

What emerged clearly from our study was that academic identity is a crucial organisational feature of disciplinary work. Aspects of academic loyalty were found to transcend both departmental and faculty arrangements and had implications for the way in which work was conceived and carried out in different settings.

One way of understanding academic identity is by linking it with ideas of purity and impurity and examining the concept of boundary which separates any given subject area from any other. The Bernstein use of boundary (at the heart of structural cultural anthropology and derived from the work of Durkheim and Mauss, see Atkinson 1985) has been a crucial tool in the present analysis.

Bernstein has applied the use of boundary in two elementary ways, generating the complementary terms classification and framing. Classification is intended to capture the strength and character of educational knowledge, whereas framing refers to educational contents and what counts as appropriate educational knowledge. Used together, these constructs enable us to compare doctoral work carried out under different disciplinary arrangements, both across disciplines and within disciplinary constraints. Classification refers primarily to curriculum/subject/discipline within the academic setting. Where classification of knowledge is strong then the academy is likely to be arranged in strongly bounded segments.

Social anthropology can be described in terms of strong classification because it constitutes a primary discipline and has a discrete subject identity. Members of anthropology departments expressed a strong sense of disciplinary membership. This identity appeared to be rooted in the essential nature of anthropological work.

Our research clearly indicated that anthropological fieldwork lies at the heart of disciplinary work and forms the root or essence of academic identity for members. Many of our anthropology respondents, like this postgraduate,[3] cited fieldwork as the key feature distinguishing anthropology from other social science disciplines:

> I think the most important thing to ask people (is) why anthropology is different from other subjects and what they think is special about it. Because it does present special problems of which as a PhD student, fieldwork stands as the central difference with other subjects.

The first point about fieldwork is that traditionally anthropological work is highly empirical. This means that members who haven't completed empirical PhDs or carried out substantial fieldwork tend to become marginalised in the discipline. So for example a supervisor suggested to us that non-empirical PhDs could not really:

---

3   We have taken great pains to try to preserve the confidentiality of all our respondents. This includes the following precautions: deliberately fudging the precise number of departments visited in any given discipline; falsifying inessential details of people's research, when quoted for illustrative purposes; avoidance of undue characterisation of particular departments; using the standard term 'PhD' even if a department prefers to use 'DPhil'; and refraining from identifying the gender of our respondents.

…exist in anthropology because it's very very exceptional not to have fieldwork as part of a PhD.

In some cases this can cause problems for staff and postgraduates not carrying out substantial pieces of fieldwork or those who are completing non-empirical or theoretical PhDs. These individuals can, and often did, find themselves marginalised within the discipline. The importance of fieldwork to anthropological careers is crucial and one reason for this is that the successful fieldwork experience is seen as a union ticket to disciplinary membership. The product of fieldwork, and particularly this applies to doctoral work, was expressed by members as cultural capital, to be exploited throughout the anthropological career:

> It's much more about acquiring this body of cultural capital than it is about acquiring an intellectual tool kit. (Supervisor)

It was not only in anthropology, as a primary discipline, where we found high levels of disciplinary identity. Disciplinary identity was found to be equally important in subject areas which have been described as multi-disciplinary in that they are made up of several different subject areas, and which we have called secondary disciplines, identified with single disciplinary allegiances. The exception to this occurred where the discipline was characterised by strong vocational orientation as in the case of town planning. In town planning disciplinary identity was derived from either the area of practice application, or couched in the more generic description of social scientist.

In secondary disciplines we looked at, we found academic identity was strongest, therefore, among members of development studies and urban studies departments and weakest amongst members of town planning departments. Where it was strong, however, disciplinary identity emanated from discipline of origin rather than discipline of destiny. It emerged clearly that academic identity was not necessarily synonymous with disciplinary identity, particularly among the secondary disciplines.

In secondary disciplines we found the relationship between academic identity and disciplinary identity to be more complex than in single disciplines such as anthropology. In secondary disciplines, departments were interdisciplinary in character in that their members were subject specialists and allegiances to their primary disciplines, or disciplines of origin, were strong.

The strength of commitment to discipline of origin owed much to the fact that it was the early socialising discipline into academia, as explained by a staff member from a development studies department:

The paradox is while we're in an interdisciplinary setting we've all actually come from single disciplines and we've all come as doctrinal students or whatever, and come to an interdisciplinary setting through a single discipline route.

Members of secondary disciplines tended to describe themselves first and foremost as subject experts with overriding interests rooted in primary academic loyalties. The majority described themselves as economists, sociologists or anthropologists working in interdisciplinary teams alongside other different, albeit complementary, subject specialists:

> I think we're the sort of people who are interested in working with colleagues in other disciplines, but... the demarcation lines between disciplines remain pretty tightly drawn.

Although interdisciplinary departments housed experts from a range of social science disciplines, each department was characterised by a body or bodies of experts from particular disciplines and tended to attract postgraduate study in those fields. Departmental members whose interests lay outside those fields tended to attract fewer postgraduate students.

Within the interdisciplinary context both staff and students tended to work from within a single disciplinary base. This was not thought to be a problem for the majority of PhD students because most of them emanated from primary disciplines and issues such as research topic, theoretical allegiance, choice of supervisor and methodology were treated accordingly. Doctoral candidates who had received their undergraduate training in a multi-disciplinary context, and saw themselves as essentially multi-disciplinary, posed more of a problem even within secondary disciplines because, as outlined by a PhD supervisor in development studies, they could not easily relate to any particular disciplinary body of knowledge:

> The more I do this job the less I believe there is any such thing as multi-disciplinary development studies. You have to come to this subject with a base and then you can make the connections out. Far too many people come either with no disciplinary base... as a result of which they're too far from the frontier of any of these disciplines to make any serious contribution. Or they come with one disciplinary base but wanting to pursue another and in the same situation. They're too far away from the frontier to say anything sensible.

This had implications for the choice of department, selection of supervisor, theoretical allegiance and methodology and could, as in the case of one student, be a source of problems for doctoral research:

The student was caught in this classic multi-disciplinary trap... (he/she was not clear whether he/she was an economist or a political scientist looking at agricultural research). And as a result of that he/she didn't really have any clear hypothesis before he started, he didn't know what he was looking at, he didn't then get the base he needed to demonstrate anything.

The primary discipline (or discipline of origin) was described by informants as important in providing a research framework from within which the student could develop his/her work. A supervisor in urban studies described how the lack of disciplinary base or framework exposed one of his/her PhD students to a range of tempting distractions;

> The exposure in a multi-disciplinary school to a variety of other exciting things distracted the student to the extent that he/she never actually was able to decide how he/she actually wanted to understand the world–whether he/she was macro, micro, sociological, policy analysis... all these are interrelated but it was quite a struggle.

The concern that doctoral students in the multi-disciplinary environment should retain a sense of disciplinary base, led some informants, like this supervisor from development studies, to encourage students to work outward from a single disciplinary core:

> My approach is to etch out in anthropology so that they actually I hope gain a grounding in anthropology and become in a sense anthropologists in this multi-disciplinary environment, but engaging with economists, political scientists or whatever.

Identification with a particular body of knowledge or subject area was found to be strongest amongst our anthropology respondents, as members of a discipline characterised by strong classification. We found therefore that disciplinary identity reflected the strength of classification, and even within weakly classified disciplines, such as development studies and urban studies, subject loyalties (to primary disciplines) tended to override multi-disciplinary (or secondary disciplinary) allegiances.

Our study has also highlighted how the style and content of academic work, for doctoral research, is informed by both institutional arrangements and features relating to disciplinary culture. In this respect we found Bernstein's construct of 'frame' a useful tool in our analysis.

Informants' accounts of what constitutes an appropriate topic or research area reflected particular research cultures indexing the various disciplines we looked at. Our research particularly indicated how disciplines differed in the extent to which research topics at doctoral level were seen as an expression of particular disciplinary traditions or, in other words, as an integral part of the essence of disciplinary work. Where doctoral work was described in terms of disciplinary tradition, framing was strongest. Where doctoral work was presented in terms of the overriding research problem or topic, then framing was at its weakest. In other words, where framing was strong there were definite boundaries which defined what counted as appropriate disciplinary work. Where framing was weaker, then disciplinary boundaries became blurred and contents were subjugated to the research task at hand.

The various disciplinary cultures ranged on a continuum. At one extreme, for example in social anthropology, the topic of a student's doctoral research was portrayed as integral to the discipline and what counted as appropriate work was seen as an expression of a particular academic tradition. To reiterate, fieldwork was seen to lie at the heart of anthropological work and informed the essence of disciplinary identity.

Central to this identity was the concept of anthropological under-standing, which is reached through the fieldwork experience. This is not, however, a process which readily lends itself to explication, but relies on tacit and implicit processes which themselves inform the character of anthropological work. In the account given below, an anthropology PhD student describes the way in which anthropology differs from other social science disciplines in the focus of its essential interests:

> If you take a thing like pig husbandry you would think it was a very straightforward thing. As an agriculturist or an economist you will think there is such a thing as pig husbandry, and we do it in a certain way. I'm going to find out how they do it and that's it. And I think as an anthropologist you have to do this, but you have to go one step further in trying to understand why they do it in the way they do it. Their rationale behind it and what kind of model of husbandry they have. And this is not done by any other discipline even if they work with the same issues under-ground. The anthropological understanding goes beyond that.

The way in which anthropological understanding is reached does not readily lend itself to explanation. Respondents' accounts were couched in vocabularies based on tacit understandings rather than any explicit criteria. Explanations were embedded in the discovery processes, which as an anthropology PhD student explains are both personal and implicit:

As an anthropologist I have my focus basically on things which are intangible... how people generate ideas and communicate them.

The centrality of fieldwork to the process of anthropological understanding was described to us by another current PhD student:

I'm also very much someone who thinks that fieldwork is very important, that we don't just sit here and imagine how things are. And although it's very hard to describe what actually happens, what status the data have that we gather in the field, you are exposed to these unsatisfactory experiences, people talk to you, they hit you on the head, they do all kinds of things to you, this is real, you have an experience, it is still very difficult to say what validity the description you bring back from the field has.

At the other extreme, in the case of town planning and to a lesser extent in the case of development studies and urban studies, doctoral research was defined primarily in terms of specific research problems, or problem solving. The problem or doctoral topic was itself portrayed in terms that were extrinsic to or separate from particular intellectual or academic interests or traditions.

In such cases, where research problems were detached or distinct from the essence of disciplinary work, disciplines were described by members as problem or policy oriented and their work was defined primarily in terms of vocational practice or policy-led research.

Two ways in which members of disciplines which were problem or policy oriented characterised their work were as follows. The first was the way in which members, like this supervisor from development studies, distanced their work from work of other departments in the institution:

This is an applied research institute with some people who have academic pretensions. In many ways we're much more like research institutes than university departments.

One obvious marker of this distancing was apparent in the way which some development studies and urban studies departments were called Research Centres and Institutes, rather than departments; their funding arrangements were partially dependent upon income raised by members through research and consultancy work, and in some cases were not UFC funded.

Secondly, and related to this, was the way in which members described their work as practical, pragmatic and related to 'real world' interests and issues. In the quotation below, for example, a member of a development studies department describes the discipline as:

...a very policy-oriented subject and the great majority of our students have a genuine interest in doing something about the world. A lot of them see the PhD as solving a particular problem.

Problem-driven departments can be contrasted to primary disciplines, which in contrast retain high levels of academic purity. Academic purity diminishes as the vocational orientation of a department increases, and this was nowhere more apparent than among members of our town planning departments:

> In recent years there's been a new breed of hybrid person I guess, who's been brought up in a discipline and like an old Catholic lapsed somewhat. And I've been exposed to interdisciplinary currents.

Doctoral work in problem-driven or policy-driven departments is therefore differentiated from more 'academically pure' disciplines like anthropology. These differences were summed up below by a supervisor from a town planning department:

> The emphasis on a theoretical core has diminished. And it's now acceptable to have a practical policy related core and for that to be the legitimate focus of the work. It can be a practically driven thesis rather than a theoretically driven one. And that's a tension in these kind of applied areas, about how the thesis is driven.

In problem-oriented departments disciplinary knowledge was harnessed to address particular and specifically defined research problems. Hence:

> In development studies more than anywhere else you bring your background disciplinary skills to bear on specific contexts.

Where problem orientation was a motivating disciplinary feature, the boundaries traditionally insulating different subject areas could become weakened as subject contents became subjugated to the overriding principle of the research problem. Some of the informants, like this supervisor from urban studies, felt that an interdisciplinary background was best suited to this kind of research:

> My preference would be to work in an interdisciplinary department but perhaps that's because I don't have a very strong sense of disciplinary base... I think if you're interested in policy then the notion of academic discipline is not so clearly defined.

Members of these departments tended to draw upon more than one disciplinary base and postgraduates were more likely to have supervisors in more than one subject area. Development studies and urban studies can be described as more outward looking than anthropology, which preserved higher levels of insulation between subject contents.

In protecting the boundaries separating it from other subjects, anthropology maintained higher levels of academic purity.

Problem orientation therefore typically characterises secondary, or multi-disciplinary, departments. These departments can be seen as a melting pot for a range of disciplinary experiences, which as we discussed earlier may create problems for doctoral students:

> I think in some ways PhDs in Development Studies are more complicated than ones in academic disciplines because there aren't established theories or methodologies.

The problems caused by lack of disciplinary base or framework, however, may be partially overcome by the importance or emphasis placed upon the research problem, around which the doctoral research revolves. As described by a development studies supervisor, the problem itself replaces disciplinary framework as the guiding principle for research work:

> The lack of a rigid framework you get from a straight discipline may be a problem. But many of our students come because they're interested in a particular problem, a real world problem as opposed to a disciplinary problem.

That is not to say that problem-oriented disciplines or departments are 'anti' academic, but their work encapsulates both academic and practical concerns. The emphasis, as described by a supervisor from urban studies, however remains rooted with the practical over the academic nature of disciplinary work:

> It can be a little bit schizophrenic. This place is very policy-oriented although there's also pure academic debate and theory, so there is a pervasive feeling that if you're not doing practical work then what are you doing here?

The emphasis on pragmatic work and policy issues was reinforced by students carrying out doctoral work under these arrangements. The doctoral student below describes why she was attracted to an urban studies department:

> I valued their (the department's) mixture of academic skills and down to earth practical concerns. They make sure their work is firmly related to good practice.

Choice of methods for doctoral research

The way in which the research topic or problem is conceived has implications for choice of, and preparation in the use of, appropriate methods at doctoral level. In the case of anthropology we found that methods were determined by the fieldwork experience and not predetermined prior to that experience. Students, like this postgraduate anthropologist, described how reflexivity is an important aspect of doing anthropological fieldwork:

> ... If one takes the image of the handyman, you go out with a pile of techniques in your mental suitcase, you don't know which one you're going to be able to use. You've no idea of the kind of situation.

The importance of anthropological understanding, as discussed earlier, is related to issues of cultural difference which means that research techniques are seen as necessarily contextually dependent. This anthropology PhD student describes how the techniques which he/she employed during the course of his/her own fieldwork were:

> ... mainly determined by constraints in the field, because when you go in and choose one subject as an anthropologist, you don't always find that it is relevant to the people among whom you're living, and you don't always call the tune as part of your methodology. You pick up on things which are important there.

A similar view is expressed by an anthropology PhD student, who contrasts anthropological fieldwork with that in another social science discipline and the implications for research training in anthropology:

> The tenor of anthropology compared to sociology is that you go and find out things without knowing what questions to ask... and that's why in a sense there's an argument for not having much training before the fieldwork.

In policy-oriented or problem-oriented departments research methods were not treated as problematic *per se*. The usefulness of different methods or techniques were evaluated in terms of their appropriateness or effectiveness in addressing the research problem. Where problems of methodology were described they were most often couched in operational or political terms.

The implications for research methods training in both primary and secondary disciplines were interesting. Both disciplinary arrangements rejected research methods training across the board, but for different reasons. In the case of anthropology, too much research preparation was felt to impede good fieldwork.

Research training

We found the extent to which disciplines tended to problematise the essential nature of the research work was in part related to the extent to which qualitative methods informed disciplinary identity. Al-

though departments differed in the importance which they attached
to the usage of qualitative methods, in common with each other they
shared the view that qualitative methods did not readily lend themselves to formal instruction because their principles defied transla-
tion into teaching formula. Here are two accounts given by
anthropology supervisors:

> The participant observation is not, I would say, a research method
> which can be taught in the classroom and applied in the field,
> whereas statistical methods can be taught in the classroom and
> applied in the field... But of course participant observation is
> hardly a method. I think it's the *sine qua non*. It's something you
> can only learn by doing.

> ...all this business of training I think is largely spurious, it's
> something that's learnt by the experience of doing it, it's rather
> like teaching music, you can't teach people to play without a
> piano, it's only by playing that they can learn, and I think field-
> work is like that.

This traditional view of fieldwork was shared by many of our informants, and is an attitude which is still prevalent, particularly among
anthropologists. Hence:

> ...fieldwork was something you did and you couldn't explain it
> any more than you could explain how you keep your balance on
> a bicycle... and something of the same anomaly seems to me to
> pertain to the notion of teaching participant observation, teaching
> how to be perceptive, teaching how not to put your foot in it
> socially, teaching how to be subtle. Because all these notions are
> culturally specific, you see.

The very nature or essence of anthropological fieldwork was trans-
lated to us in terms of tacit and personal experiences:

> The debate over fieldwork experience, the way knowledge is
> constructed out of observation, interaction between the inform-
> ant and the investigator, the general reflexivity of the process is
> very much the stuff of the training before going into the
> field... there remains a certain mystique about (it). Yes, in order to
> do the *rite de passage* properly you've got to do it by yourself.

At its extreme this view, as expressed by a PhD student in anthropology, supported the idea that training in methods hindered good
anthropological fieldwork:

> ...this may be heretical, but I think a lot of these research courses
> can impede good research.

In not only research but also in evaluation, anthropology was described by its members as a personal and subjective experience:

I think it's a discipline that rests very much on opinion and interpretation and very little on established methodologies. So there aren't any criteria for judging anyone, except what you personally feel about their work.

and specifically relating to the evaluation of PhD work:

... in other words we don't have a lot of criteria we're looking for, that exists on a conscious level. But in practice we end up with implicit or unconscious ideas that we're looking for.

The same view was not held to be true of quantitative methods, or their formal instruction. The majority of respondents across departments felt that instruction in quantitative methods was both important and desirable. However the appropriateness of instruction in quantitative techniques was felt, by our respondents, to be in direct ratio to the requirements of particular research projects and the related needs of postgraduate students. This was summed up nicely by a supervisor in a development studies department:

... if there's a research proposal which turns out to require a technique they don't have, they'll have to acquire it on their own with whatever help we can offer, but I'm not going to waste their time by assuming they all need the same techniques.

In town planning particularly it was felt that postgraduate students would already possess adequate experience in required research methods:

Planning is about methods of researching things, that's what planners do. So this research stuff is talked about like a shopping list of methods, and we say 'they've probably done this at undergraduate level'.

Although training in quantitative methods was seen as both desirable and necessary, at the same time PhD students were intolerant of methods training for training's sake rather than as a means to an end. This is illustrated by an evaluation of methods training provided by a town planning postgraduate:

I know people who went on research methods courses and it was OK but didn't teach them anything in detail. I think it assumed no knowledge and started from a very general level, whereas some people already have basic knowledge.

This view was reinforced by a supervisor in a town planning department:

I see it very much a learning of skills and attitudes that will make practice better. I don't see any benefit in research for its own sake.

And if they're taking a subject of practical value to the outside world, that's also important.

Again we found that relevance to their own particular practical work was the yardstick which students primarily used to assess the appropriateness of their methods training:

> The research methods course was an MSc course, but it didn't teach me anything new. It wasn't practical enough. I should have done a computer course, but I didn't and I'm having problems with that now actually.

Where methods training was felt to assist in addressing research problems then it was applauded by staff members and supported in the students' accounts. Once again it was the potential contribution towards practice which was used as a yardstick to evaluate training:

> Also as part of their (the PhD students) training they take the research methods course, which is offered to all students. So we train them both to be confident in terms of research techniques and on top of that their research findings are of credibility when it comes to implementing their work. Urban design is never completely theoretical work, it always has some practical implications.

Similarly in town planning a discipline characteristically reliant upon quantitative techniques, methods training was an acceptable element of doctoral work. Where appropriate training was not available, students expressed grievance:

> At the moment I'm doing quantitative work using stats packages to look at the data, in my questionnaire survey, and I'm having to rely on the people who do computing in the department to do that work for me because I've had no training in the use of packages so I can't do that on my own.

The traditional dependence upon, or preference for, quantitative methods apparent in town planning departments could cause problems for students intending to carry out more qualitative work. In the case of this student, training in qualitative methods was not so readily available:

> If you mention research methods they assume you mean regression analysis. In my first year I sat in on a computer course and found it really irrelevant to what I was doing, to the data I had. I felt I needed something more a social science based computer course. So the whole notion of what constitutes a research method was based on a positivist view, natural science, quantitative. As if there is a scientific method which could be easily transposed over to social scientific research.

Discussion

Two constructs that we have found particularly useful in this analysis are classification and frame. When used together these constructs enable us to understand how our respondents, across and within disciplines, identify with bodies of academic knowledge and the way in which educational contents are seen as appropriate to disciplinary work at doctoral level.

The research has shown that disciplinary identity is an important function of the organisation of academic work across departments, disciplines and subject areas. The source of this identity was most often found to be rooted in members' discipline of origin, the exception to this being in highly vocationally organised disciplines such as town planning (where identities tended to be couched either in 'practice' terms or generic academic descriptions).

The importance of academic identity is that it informs the way in which disciplinary work is conceived and carried out. Where disciplines, as in the case of anthropology, are strongly classified or, in other words, well insulated from other subject areas, we found that disciplinary identity and academic loyalty to the subject area were strong. Boundaries defining what counted as anthropological work were rigorously maintained by members. In this sense we found anthropology was more strongly framed (or academically pure) than the other disciplines which we visited.

In the secondary disciplines, urban studies, development studies and town planning, classification and framing were weaker as boundaries between different constituent subject areas were blurred. In these disciplines educational contents were subjugated to the overriding principle of the research problem.

The strength of boundaries between subject areas and disciplines, coupled with the extent to which members described themselves as problem or policy (or in the case of town planning, vocationally) driven was found in turn to have implications for attitudes towards particular methods and the appropriateness for methods training at doctoral level.

The different departments which we have studied were characterised by reliance upon preferred methods. Two concepts which have been crucial to our analysis are 'indeterminacy' and 'technicality', developed by Jamous and Peloille (1970) as a classificatory device for understanding different types of professional work.

Whereas technical knowledge can be described as that part of occupational work which lends itself to documentation, and at its extreme can be portrayed as a list of specifications whose mastery relies upon memory and/or physical dexterity, indeterminacy implies a kind of tacit knowledge which remains the personal property of the practitioner. Whereas technical knowledge lends itself to formalised instruction, aspects of indeterminate knowledge defy translation into a teaching formula because they are intuitive rather than learnt.

Our research suggests that whereas technicality indexes quantitative methods, indeterminacy indexes qualitative work. From the data it is apparent that disciplinary work is characterised by different levels of both indeterminacy and technicality in the same way in which both elements are represented in different forms of occupational work (Atkinson, Reid and Sheldrake 1977).

Reliance on qualitative methods, plus the opinion of our respondents that qualitative methods are unteachable, determined the extent to which disciplinary work could be described as indeterminate. Therefore anthropology was, with its traditional reliance upon ethnographic method, the most indeterminate of the disciplines under discussion here.

The reliance upon qualitative methods varied from discipline to discipline but we found shared understandings about the nature of qualitative work. Although departments were characterised by field-work location, whether abroad or at home, ideas about cultural differences were implicit in qualitative methods. Cultural difference implied elements of both strangeness and unpredictability which in turn informed methods of application. Anthropological methods, for example, were described as contextually dependent and choice of research techniques was therefore determined by constraints in the field rather than being imposed from outside. This contrasts with work carried out in more problem-oriented disciplines like development studies where techniques are dependent upon demands and constraints of the research project.

Because of the unpredictable element in qualitative fieldwork, predetermined research strategies were felt to hinder rather than assist data collection. Good students were those who maintained an open and flexible approach to data collection and good research projects were those which developed in the field through the experience of the fieldworker.

Implicit in the belief that research strategies cannot be anticipated was the idea that fieldwork necessitated employing skills outside the accepted range of research techniques. These skills were described in terms of the personal qualities of the researcher, such as empathy and reflexivity.

The unpredictable and highly personal element of qualitative data collection meant fieldwork was celebrated as a highly subjective experience which did not lend itself easily to objective evaluation. At one extreme, in anthropology, data collection period was seen by many respondents as a *rite de passage* and as such to be experienced uniquely by the practitioner as an 'ordeal by fire'. Although this traditional attitude towards anthropological fieldwork differed between departments, we did find it extended to home PhD students working in Britain. During the fieldwork duration these students tended to keep away from the academy and had limited (if any) contact with supervisors. We found anthropological 'ordeal by fire' approach to fieldwork characterised departments which were most traditionally academic. Where anthropology was more development-oriented then data collection was not treated as a personal experience to the same extent. For example, PhD anthropology students working in development were more likely to receive supervisory visits in the field and in some instances work as part of a regional specialist team as opposed to in isolation.

The indeterminate essence of qualitative work informed attitudes to its formal instruction. In the case of quantitative work attitudes to training were positive, to the extent which training was geared to specific needs of research problems. Because the specific needs applying to qualitative fieldwork were seen to defy anticipation, relying more upon the reflexivity of the researcher, training in qualitative methods was largely felt to be inappropriate. Although research needs were equally specific they were not felt to address a predetermined problem but rather problems which arose out of, and were specific to the fieldwork experience *per se*.

References

Atkinson, P.A. (1983) The reproduction of the professional community. In R. Dingwall and P. Lewis (eds) *The Sociology of the Professions*. London: Macmillan.

Atkinson, P.A. (1985) *Language, Structure and Reproduction: An Introduction to the Sociology of Basil Bernstein*. London: Methuen.

Atkinson, P.A. (1991) Decoding Bernstein. *Sociological Review 39*, 3, 647–54.

Atkinson, P.A. and Delamont, S. (1985) Teacher socialisation: the research which lost its way. *The British Journal of the Sociology of Education, 6*, 3, 307–322.

Atkinson, P.A., Reid, M.E. and Sheldrake, P.F. (1977) Medical mystique. *Sociology of Work and Occupations, 4*, 3, 243–280.

Becker, H.S., Geer, B., Hughes, E.C. and Strauss, A.L. (1961) *Boys in White*. Chicago: University of Chicago Press.

Bernstein, B. (1977) *Class, Codes and Control Vol 3*. London: Routledge.

Bernstein, B. (1990) *Class, Codes and Control Vol 4*. London: Routledge.

Bloom, S.W. (1973) *Power and Dissent in the Medical School*. New York: Free Press.

Bourdieu, P. (1988) *Homo Academicus*. Cambridge: Polity Press.

Bourdieu, P. and Passeron, J.C. (1977) *Reproduction in Education, Society and Culture*. London: Sage.

Haas, J. and Shaffir, W. (1977) The professionalisation of medical students: developing competence and a cloak of competence. *Symbolic Interaction*, 1, 77–88.

Haas, J. and Shaffir, W. (1987) Becoming Doctors. Greenwich, CT: JAI Press.

Jamous, H. and Peloille, B. (1970) Professions or self-perpetuating system? In J.A. Jackson (ed) *Professions and Professionalisation*. Cambridge: Cambridge Univeristy Press.

Parry, O. (1991) The production and reproduction of news: Broadcast students at journalism school. *International Journal of Qualitative Studies in Education*, 4, 3, 215–230.

Robbins, D. (1991) *The Work of Pierre Bourdieu*. Milton Keynes: Open University Press.

Shuval, J. (1975) Socialisation of health professionals in Israel: Early sources of congruence and differentiation. *Journal of Medical Education*, 50, 443–457.

Chapter 4

Research Students and Their Supervisors in Education and Psychology

Tim Hill, Sandra Acker and Edith Black

Concern has been rising in both Britain and North America about PhD completion rates and the spectre of an insufficient supply of new scholars for the maintenance of the academic enterprise (Bowen and Rudenstine 1992, Bowen and Sosa 1989). Most of the literature singles out the relationship of supervisor and student as a critical influence on the completion of the doctorate. Supervision is said to be 'crucial' (Burnett 1977 p.17, Phillips and Pugh 1987 p.22) Wright and Lodwick 1989 p.37–46); 'pivotal' (Council of Graduate Schools 1991 p.22); 'at the heart of most research training' (Williams, 1988 p.6); 'at the core of the project' (Connell 1985 p.41); 'the single most important variable affecting the success of the research process' (ESRC 1991 p.8). It also appears to be exceptionally difficult: 'the most complex and subtle form of teaching in which we engage' (Brown and Atkins 1988 p.115); 'probably the most responsible task undertaken by an academic' (Burnett 1977 p.17).

Such testimonies seem curiously at odds with the general dearth of research on the detailed nature of supervision (Brown and Atkins 1988) as well as persistent suspicions that universities neglect research students (Welsh 1982) and make little attempt to train academic staff to supervise (Council of Graduate Schools 1991). A particular concern has been the relatively low rates of thesis submission in the social sciences (Winfield 1987). As a consequence of this concern, the Economic and Social Research Council (ESRC) introduced a policy whereby students awarded grants would not be permitted to study at departments with poor submission rates.

This policy appears to have produced dramatic rises among full-time, grant-supported students in the number of PhDs completed within four years. Other moves towards increasing accountability and providing systematic, compulsory research training for students have since been made (ESRC 1991).

The ESRC has also made efforts to remedy the lack of research on the social science research student experience by commissioning a number of projects. Four of these are qualitative studies, including our own. Our focus is on the supervisory process, which we see as a teaching–learning interaction which takes place in particular disciplinary, departmental, institutional and national contexts.

This chapter provides an overview of our major findings. After a brief description of the study, we review the arrangements departments made for their research students. Next we look at the context in which supervision takes place: the workload of supervisors and their preparation for the task; the diversity of the student body; the conceptions of the PhD that mark the disciplines studied. We then turn to the heart of the supervisory process, examining questions and dilemmas concerning the conduct of tutorials; the style of supervision; relationships and responsibilities of students and supervisors. Finally, we report some student reflections on their experience and conclude by noting theoretical and policy implications of the study.

The study

The study is an interview-based exploration of supervisory practices, concentrating on supervisors, research students and key personnel in three psychology and three education departments in three universities. Departments were carefully selected so as to produce, within each discipline, a range of both sizes and UFC ratings. It was intended that the design should be capable of yielding fruitful contrasts both between the two disciplines and between the three institutions in terms of their management of postgraduate research students.

The research questions were informed by the available literature on the supervision of research students and an ERIC literature search was also carried out in order to extend our coverage into American material. Semi-structured interview schedules were devised for key personnel (e.g. Heads of Department and Tutors for Research Students), supervisors and research students.

An informal approach was made to each proposed department, followed up by a preliminary visit by one of the project co-directors, during which both the Head of Department and the Tutor for Research Students were interviewed. Relevant documentary data such as prospectuses, student handbooks, blank application forms and student lists were collected. Field notes were taken. These data were used to make preliminary decisions on the sample of students and supervisors to be interviewed. The aim was to include approximately twelve supervisors of differing levels of experience and twelve students of various types and at differing stages of their research in each department, adjusted according to the size of the department and to the number of members of staff actually involved in supervision. In all, 62 supervisors and 87 students were interviewed.

On the preliminary visit a timetable was established with each department for the second, more intensive, period of fieldwork. Interviews were the main method of data collection in this second stage. The blocks of time (3 or 4 weeks per department) which the researcher spent in the field facilitated participation in the formal and informal life of the departments. Field notes were also made during these visits. With the agreement of the respondents, interviews were tape-recorded and later transcribed. Transcripts were then analysed using 'The Ethnograph', computer software for the analysis of qualitative data.

Departmental practices

Admissions and matching

Departments were asked to describe their administrative procedures for the admission of research students. Each department had one member of the academic staff who carried responsibility for these procedures. The responsibility rotated and was usually held for three or four years. The title attached to this person varied but we refer to them as Tutors for Research Students or simply Tutors. All departments had well-established procedures for handling the relevant documents from initial enquiry to acceptance or rejection. Tutors readily described these processes and provided us with the associated documentation.

Fundamental to the admissions procedure was the process of matching a student with a supervisor. Tutors in psychology departments had sharper mental maps of the boundaries of colleagues' research interest than did Tutors in education departments, but all began their search for student/supervisor compatibility at the level of common research interests. Supervisors, too, invoked the notion of an identifiable field of expertise, when asked what factors would lead them to accept or reject a potential research student. In a few cases, supervisors reported arm-twisting: 'someone had to do it'. Matching was not always easily accomplished, nor did it take any account of preferences for directive or other supervisory styles. One Tutor described the process as the 'weak point' in the admissions procedures.

Students too began their search for an appropriate supervisor at the level of academic interest, although they were rather more interested in personal compatibility than were the supervisors. We found it useful to distinguish between 'cold' and 'warm' entry. Students with 'cold' entry had no prior knowledge of a department apart from the information given to them at the point of initial enquiry. Their applications then went through admissions procedures which rested on the matching of research interests. Other students had followed a course in the department before embarking on a research degree and had some prior knowledge, not only of the research interests of the staff, but also of the way in which they worked. Their entry was 'warm', circumventing the 'weak point' in the process.

Arrangements for supervision

There was considerable variation between and within departments in the arrangements for supervision. We were provided with lists of research students which indicated who was responsible for the supervision of each student. Reality was often at variance with what the lists indicated.

Where two supervisors were listed for a student we found a range of practices, even within the same department. At one extreme students talked about one of their two listed supervisors as a 'phantom' supervisor; someone they had last seen at initial interview or, briefly, in the early stages. In two psychology departments the Tutor for Research Students was listed as second supervisor. This was done mainly to formalise the pastoral aspects of the Tutor's role but students were often unaware of the reasons for this practice. In one education department a member of staff with considerable expertise in the computer-aided analysis of quantitative data was second supervisor to a surprisingly large number of students. However, we discovered that his role was that of a consultant who was available when necessary. Generally, across all six departments, there were mixed feelings about whether supervision is best performed as a single or as a joint task. There were some examples of truly joint supervision in which two supervisors would divide the responsibility for different elements of a student's thesis, having either occasional or regular triangular meetings. Examples of this mode were rare, but were considered successful and advantageous by both the students and supervisors involved. In practice most students were dependent on a single supervisor.

Research training

The general picture was one of universities making positive responses to the training needs of their research students with all departments offering courses in research methods. Some training was provided on a faculty basis and some on a departmental basis. One of the universities ran a series of long and short courses for all new research students in the social sciences. It was more common though for research training to be provided by individual departments. Two education departments made relevant courses on taught master's programmes available to research students and the third was planning to do so in the following academic year. In all three psychology departments students who felt the need to do so were encouraged to sit in on third year undergraduate courses in statistical methods. One of the education departments with a large number of part-time students provided a three day course in research methods timed to coincide with the local schools' half-term holiday.

Training at the departmental level most commonly took the form of regular seminars. These were organised by staff but were led by both staff and students and sometimes by visiting academics. Generally students expressed appreciation of whatever was offered to them by way of research training although some criticisms were expressed. Full-time students, particularly in psychology, were likely to complain of the time taken up by attendance at seminars not seen as relevant to their own research. Part-time students who were employed full-time outside the university experienced difficulties in attending courses and seminars because of their timing and sometimes because of the lengthy travelling involved.

Material resources

We asked the Tutors and the students to describe the material resources available to research students. We also asked the students whether they found the provision adequate. With only a few exceptions, there was a general consensus that the provision of such resources as libraries, computer access, photocopying and telephones was adequate. All departments provided work space for full-time students, usually on a shared basis with other students. Some found that sharing diminished the sense of isolation while others found it disturbing.

There were interesting variations in the allocation and use of social space. All three psychology departments had an area designated as a common room with drinks available. In two this space was open to everybody in the department while in the third undergraduates were excluded. A common complaint from psychology research students was that the social space was not fully used. Most staff and research students were identified with a research group and tended to stay in the part of the department where their research facilities were based. These social arrangements meant that most full-time psychology students had frequent, informal contact with their supervisor. In two education departments there was a clear demarcation of social space between staff and students. Staff, academic, administrative and secretarial, were in one common room while all categories of student shared another. The third education department had a small room with a drinks machine, which was seldom used by anyone. The social arrangements in education departments meant that contacts between students and supervisors were less often informal occasions and students had less of a chance to participate in an academic community.

Monitoring progress

Supervisors in all departments were expected to complete regular reports on each student at intervals varying from 6 to 12 months. Departments also had arrangements for upgrading students from MPhil to PhD status. In practice these varied from an occasion similar to a *viva voce* examination involving other academics to an informal assessment by the supervisor acting alone.

Context

Supervisors' work

For most university teachers the supervision of research students is just one of a variety of tasks which they undertake. We were keen to explore the place of research student supervision within the general work-pattern of staff. We asked them to make an assessment of the amount of time they spent on each of the four categories of work: teaching, research, administration and other professional activities. Work patterns varied enormously. In only one department did staff mention a departmental norm. Most staff in that department were careful to explain how their work pattern did not quite follow this supposed 'norm', but it was commonly described as 2/5 teaching, 2/5 research and 1/5 administration.

Education departments tended to be characterised by a concern for initial teacher training and/or in-service professional development for teachers whereas psychology departments tended to be dominated by the pressure of undergraduate teaching. For some individuals in each discipline it was contract research and its demands which drove their working lives. Interviewees often suggested that supervision was peripheral to the reward systems of their institutions and that research and publication brought greater kudos.

Learning to be a supervisor

We asked all supervisors how they had learned to supervise. Few mentioned either being offered, or seeking, advice from colleagues. It appears that all of our supervisors learned on the job by trial and error:

> (It was) learning by doing – I know it would be frowned on nowadays but in fact I never attended any courses here on teaching us to teach, maybe you can be taught these things.

A number of the supervisors, including some of the more experienced supervisors, had no research degree themselves which meant that they had no first-hand experience of being a research student. One such supervisor told us that he felt that supervision as a task had 'just been dropped' on him and that there seemed to be an expectation that he was capable of doing it effectively simply by virtue of having been appointed to the post of university lecturer. The majority, however, were able to draw upon their own experience of being supervised, enabling them to empathise with the students. Some used their own supervisor as a role model, either a positive or, more often, a negative one:

> I had a supervisor who was very electrifying in that he maintained an interest in the subject. But I don't think it's unfair to him to say that we always seemed to finish up talking about his problems rather than mine. And I found it extremely difficult to get him to read anything because he was so busy on his own things. So I always fool myself that I wouldn't fall into that trap.

All three universities provided courses for the professional development of academics but these rarely focused upon the task of supervising research students. Such courses were invariably mentioned somewhat apologetically by staff who had heard about, rather than attended, them. There seemed to be a growing unease with the absence of any form of training in supervision though education departments tended to be more inclined to a belief in the potential value of professional development for staff than were psychology departments.

An interesting development in one department was the recent introduction of joint supervision with the specific intention of supporting staff who were inexperienced in supervision. The scheme sought to systematise the learning of supervision skills by teaming an inexperienced supervisor with a more experienced colleague:

> We have joint supervision now as a matter of course, and the joint supervisor does not have to be an expert in the field, but is an experienced person. There's a sort of sitting by Nellie aspect to it.

In view of the way that supervisors learn to supervise 'on the hoof', as one of them put it, we ascertained just how much experience of supervising research students staff actually had. We found that throughput was so small in even the biggest departments that most supervisors had seen only a small number of PhD students through to completion. Of the 62 supervisors in our sample only 9 had seen 10 or more students through to completion, 24 had supervised fewer than 6 students to completion while a further 10 supervisors had yet to supervise any students to completion. These figures prompt the disturbing thought that if supervisors are largely learning to supervise by trial and error and have so few students upon whom to practise, then many of the students are destined to be guinea pigs.

Student diversity

The experience of being a research student, even when limited to the social sciences, is not homogeneous. Other research (e.g. Acker 1992, Taylerson 1984) suggests gender may be an important differentiator, especially as most supervisors are male (although we oversampled women supervisors) while many students are female. Gender issues were seldom mentioned spontaneously by interviewees, which may indicate a low level of consciousness rather than the irrelevance of the issues. We hope to return to this topic in subsequent work.

Another major division can be drawn between 'home' students and 'overseas' students. We included students from the European Community in the latter category for the purposes of this study since they share the problems of cultural dislocation and language differences. In every department we interviewed at least one overseas student in order to capture something of the flavour of that experience. However, our main focus is upon the variety of experience as it exists among home students.

Each of the six departments provided us with lists of students. In every department part-time students outnumbered home full-time students. We noted that full-time ESRC students were in a minority in each department. Their representation ranged from 0 to 11 per cent.

Within the part-time category we discovered a variety of experience which led us to describe some part time students as 'detached' and others as 'semi-detached'. Part-time 'detached' students are more often found in education than in psychology departments and they typically have a full-time job outside the university. For the majority of these students, the thesis topic is related to some aspect of their professional development. Compared with full-time students they have little contact with the university apart from tutorials. Part-time 'semi-detached' students are more often found in psychology departments and are typically employed within the department, usually as a Research Assistant (RA) on a funded project. They thus have a dual relationship with their supervisor since he or she is usually the director of the research project on which the student is employed as an RA.

The nature and purpose of the PhD

The two disciplines were characterised by differing conceptions of the nature and purpose of the PhD. Psychology supervisors were closer to the orthodox view of the PhD as primarily a means of preparing the next generation of academics by giving them the research skills that an academic needs and by initiating them into the academic way of life:

> A PhD is primarily training for a research career. Now that's an old fashioned view, I think the PhD may be changing its character. With full-time PhDs I am training future academics. They don't all go on to be academics but that's what's at the back of my mind – they're our seed corn.

However, several expressed doubts about how sustainable such a view was in the face of the labour market for academics.

Education supervisors were more likely to mention a variety of purposes and less likely to stress the preparation of future academics. Education research students were often described as simply being interested in researching a particular problem, often one which arose from their work as teachers, or wishing to pursue a higher qualification than the taught master's degree. Referring to the prospect of an academic career, an education supervisor said:

> The people who come for our doctorates don't want that. They want to do a doctorate because they are interested in a problem. We're in a different ball game.

A number of respondents observed that the PhD had changed in recent years and some of these changes were attributed to pressure from the ESRC for high submission rates. The most commonly identified changes were the increased emphasis on the training element and the restriction of the scope of the research project in order to improve the student's chances of completion on time. As a psychology supervisor remarked:

The monitoring has become tighter and I think that's made people less adventurous because we are continually looking out for completion rates.

Process

The tutorial

Both students and supervisors were asked about such matters as how often tutorials were held and how long they lasted, who instigated a tutorial and set its agenda, and what normally happened in a tutorial.

With full-time students many supervisors timetabled a regular weekly session. In some cases this timetable was rigidly adhered to, in others it was varied according to the stage the research had reached. With part-time students the pattern was more diverse. Only one department mentioned a rule about the frequency of meetings with part-time students. In this department the onus was on students to meet with their supervisor at least six times a year.

Interesting differences emerged in student and supervisor perceptions of frequency and duration, regardless of discipline. Supervisors most often stated that meetings took place weekly or fortnightly for full-timers and monthly for part-timers, whereas students most often reported monthly and two-monthly intervals respectively. Supervisors also recalled longer-lasting tutorials of one or two hours, compared to students' reports of thirty to sixty minutes.

A number of students commented on how busy their supervisors appeared to be:

> And I think there's a problem about getting hold of one's supervisor anyway because in recent years people in that position have become busier and busier anyway.

Although only a minority of students complained of lack of contact with their supervisors, when dissatisfaction was expressed it tended to be strong:

> The academics in this place are too busy to worry about me. I've never been refused a slot but he just doesn't have the time. I don't know how he does it, I thought I worked hard but I guess he works more and so when I look at that I really don't want to press him and so I send in quite a few papers to him. Really I guess that it's like a correspondence course. I honestly think it's a burden to them.

The theme of 'busyness' is also found in some of the literature (Friedman 1977). It could be seen as a form of 'impression management' and as an attempt by academics to control their work process.

But sometimes students were the ones who avoided tutorials. Nor did all supervisors project a busy image, some maintaining an 'open door' policy. Such accessibility was appreciated by students who were fortunate enough to experience it:

I've virtually open access to David. I can just go and see him anytime I want. I don't have any formal sessions at the moment but for the first two years I did. We used to meet at least once a week, then it kind of went to once a fortnight in the second year and now it's kind of I just contact him when I need him.

Students, almost without exception, saw the agenda for the tutorial as being set by themselves, whereas supervisors most frequently reported that it was jointly negotiated. Some students experienced this responsibility as something of a shock after the structure which they had experienced as undergraduates. Channell (1990) notes this phenomenon for overseas students, even those who had previously studied in the same department on a taught course. Our data suggest that the disorientation may occur in home students too who had been accustomed to the greater degree of externally imposed structure of a taught course.

Descriptions of what took place in a tutorial were remarkably consistent between both disciplines and between students and supervisors. Both students and supervisors saw tutorials as consisting essentially of reviewing the student's work, discussing problems which had arisen in their research and planning future work.

Typically the focus of tutorials shifted as the student progressed, from discussions of designing research and locating appropriate literature to problems associated with data collection and analysis and to considerations arising from writing-up. As the student's knowledge of the field increased, the giving of references often became more reciprocal. Apart from the more frequent mentions of experiments and a greater tendency to have quantitative data in psychology, there was little discernible difference between the two disciplines in the stages described.

There was a high level of agreement amongst students on what constituted good supervision. Students valued interested feedback, constructive discussion, guidance, and suggestions about how to develop their research. A good tutorial was also one where students were made to feel that what they were doing was worthwhile. Such positive reinforcement was often mentioned by students as being important in maintaining their motivation:

I always leave on an up rather than a down – You don't feel like giving up when you come out. You might feel like giving up when you go in but when you come out you think 'Oh well, yes' and (you are) quite eager to do the next one.

Structure v independence

We asked supervisors about the extent to which they adopted a directive style with their research students. This topic highlighted a tension or dilemma for many, who saw the PhD process as entailing the production of scholars capable of independent work, yet found that many research students needed a degree of direction to complete satisfactorily and on time. Indeed there is some evidence that directive supervision gets results in terms of completed theses (Wright and Lodwick 1989). In a study by Rudd (1985) in which student 'failures' were interviewed, he reports that the idea that they might have discussed with a supervisor how to phase their work over three years or drawn up a timetable 'came as a surprising novelty to many of them' (p.81). One of the more widely-read advice books aimed at research students and their supervisors (Phillips and Pugh 1987) stresses the importance of supervisors setting deadlines, real or made up for the purpose. Supervisors, they comment, find it hard to understand that students may not be able to create their own structure.

Supervisors demonstrated differing preferences or inclinations when discussing the balance between structure and independence. A few were like the education supervisor who said, 'I'm directive, structured and very, very tasky'. Strongly directive approaches to supervision were sometimes criticised as 'spoon-feeding' by less directive colleagues. Rather more supervisors saw themselves as being non-directive in their approach to students though some of these expressed a certain regret that in the case of some students they felt that the freedom which they offered had to be somewhat circumscribed. Several spoke of having been 'fortunate' in having students who did not need a great deal of direction, one referring to it as a 'luxury'.

Underlying this tension is the issue of who 'owns' the research project. A number of supervisors regarded direction on their part as somehow incompatible with their view of the research as being owned by the student. Supervisors who de-emphasised direction were also concerned not to destroy the creative process inherent in successful research by imposing a rigid schema:

By over-structuring it you might stunt the research student – I mean the research has got to be the student's research when all's said and done, and one wouldn't want it any other way.

This view is noted by Kiely (1982) and Bargar and Duncan (1982) and was echoed by virtually all of the students who, although they expected guidance and advice from their supervisor, nonetheless saw the research as rightly their property.

While supervisors may have a preference for a certain degree of freedom or direction most stressed that the balance in any particular case depended on the student's perceived need for direction and the stage which he or she had reached in the research:

> My feeling about working with research students is there are certain elements of structure that are important in the early stages, getting people started, giving people achievable targets early on. Well defined and manageable targets like producing literature reviews and the first experiment, it's a kind of milestone.

Most supervisors answered our questions about their supervisory style by referring to individual cases and recounting how their approach had been modified to suit what they perceived as the individual student's needs:

> She needed the security of a regular structure of dates and times for supervisions and the agreement between us about just what work she was going to do in between.

Furthermore a number of the more experienced supervisors spoke of how they had made conscious alterations to their practices over the years as they had discovered that some approaches were more effective than others:

> Actually, I've become a much better supervisor and I think that's partly due to students who made demands on me. I think I'm fairly systematic and organised now.

Others referred to changes in their practice as a response to external pressures such as an increasing emphasis on completion rates following the advent of the ESRC's sanctions policy, combined with the accumulation of experience on their own part:

> I've become more structured I think, more goal oriented. I'm not sure whether that would have happened quite so much had it not been for the problems about completion rates and such like. I've grown older and perhaps wiser and the system has changed at the same time.

In all cases the change reported was invariably a move towards being more directive.

We concluded, unlike Wright (1991), that it is probably not helpful to conceive of supervisors as having a particular supervisory style independent of circumstances, for the concept of style implies a greater degree of uniformity and stability of approach to the supervisory process than we found to be the case.

The 'good' student

There was a wide consensus amongst supervisors about the qualities of a 'good' student. The ideal student is a person who is intelligent, well-informed about the area of interest, and who has certain interpersonal and technical skills including an ability to write. Supervisors repeatedly stressed that these were necessary rather than sufficient conditions. Certain personal qualities were also widely deemed to be essential ingredients. Independence, perseverance, enthusiastic curiosity, and an energetic and systematic application to the work in hand were all frequently recurring components of supervisors' typifications of the good student. Some supervisors stressed that persistence and reliability were more important than sheer intellectual brilliance.

The nature of the relationship

Both supervisors and students were asked about the nature of their relationship. We were interested in the extent to which the relationship was close and friendly or distant and cold and whether each was satisfied with that state of affairs.

For both students and supervisors the relationship was work-based and work-focused. The extent to which it extended beyond work varied according to a variety of factors which included the inclinations of both parties, the extent of rapport and the opportunities available. Chances for social interaction were most obviously restricted for part-time 'detached' students.

The majority of supervisors saw themselves as friendly and approachable whilst maintaining in most cases a certain professional distance. As one education supervisor explained, the experience of doing a PhD was not intended to be a 'trial by ordeal' and he tried to be 'affable'. Others went further and saw friendly approachability as an essential part of the teaching–learning relationship. This view was often echoed by students who said they felt more confident in expressing their own ideas when they had a friendly relationship with their supervisor:

> I can generate ideas much more if I'm feeling comfortable with someone. I feel more confident about saying 'Well, what about this?' I can handle it if he says 'Well, no that's pretty stupid really.' But if this person is quite distant then I'm not about to put my idea on the line just in case they get hammered down and I feel about this big.

Supervisors frequently indicated that they sought some limitation upon the extent of the relationship and the demands which might be made upon them. A female education supervisor thought there was a 'boundary to professional involvement' while a psychology supervisor said he had been 'lucky' that his research students had not presented him with any personal problems of the type 'one encounters with undergraduates'.

A number of students, most often in education, described the relationship as 'professional', i.e., while friendly and informal, it was nonetheless largely confined to issues to do with the work. One such student told us that he regarded the social distance as a desirable state of affairs since it avoided getting 'side-tracked' into unproductive discussions. That the relationship was seen as work-based was evident in the number of supervisors who referred to research students as being essentially colleagues, albeit junior colleagues.

Induction into academic life

We found differences between the two disciplines in the extent to which supervisors initiated their students into aspects of academic life such as conference presentations, publication and joining of learned societies. There was more evidence in psychology departments than in education departments of students being encouraged to write papers for publication, often jointly with the supervisor. The majority of psychology supervisors indicated that they regarded such initiation into academic life as an integral part of their role as supervisors.

Education students were more likely to be in the part-time 'detached' category and their supervisors sometimes expressed reservations about encouraging them to write papers before completing their theses lest it should distract them. This view was echoed by the students, some of whom said that they would consider publishing papers after completion.

The experience in retrospect

We asked all of the students to reflect upon the experience of being a research student. There were no totally negative responses; most balanced any difficulties they had encountered against what had been learned or gained from the experience.

Full-time students were more inclined to be critical of all aspects of being a research student than were either category of part-time students. Anxiety about financial problems had coloured the experience of many full-time students. We found that the nearer they were to completion, the more anxious and ambivalent they were about their future financial and career prospects in the academic world. One full-time psychology student told us:

> I'm getting out before I get seduced, staying here for ever and rotting away. I just want to live a less stressful life with a bit more space and fewer demands.

Full-timers also complained about heavy pressures to complete quickly and contradictory expectations that they also attend courses and research seminars.

Part-time 'detached' students were notably less critical of the experience than other groups. The most common cause for complaint was that they were unable to devote more time to their research. They were sympathetic to the supervisor's difficulties with competing pressures and glad of the time he or she could provide. They stressed the value to them of the process of doing the doctorate rather than its pay-off in career terms. As one such student remarked:

> And, yes, I have no regrets on that. One of the best decisions I ever made. Changes your life, research.

Part-time 'semi-detached' students earned a salary and so were not subject to the financial problems of full-timers. As they worked in their departments, they were not isolated like their 'detached' counterparts. They often had a close working relationship with their supervisor-cum-project director yet they suffered anxiety as they were not part of either staff or student hierarchies:

> You see, in that position I wasn't a member of staff really and I wasn't a student either, so I was between the two camps. And I wasn't a member of the administrative staff, so they didn't want me either.

Their project directors seemed unsure how to switch to the supervisor role and the mutual embarrassment, together with the pressure of work, led students to de-emphasise the thesis and avoid scheduling tutorials.

Conclusions

Underlying themes

Our theoretical approach was a broadly symbolic interactionist one, drawing upon American literature on professional socialisation associated with writers such as Everett Hughes and Howard Becker, as well as contemporary British sociology of education. The supervisory process, we believe, is best conceptualised as a form of teaching learning. As such, it is subject to negotiation and change. Both supervisor and student responses confirmed the latter point, supervisors being at pains to describe the modifications made in style to meet what they saw as students' needs; students explaining how they either pushed the supervisor to work differently or, more often, tailored their expectations to fit what was on offer. The matching process itself, although presented as a rational series of steps, was only partially successful, being influenced by gaps in information about prospective students, limits to what supervisor research specialities could be found within a department; academics' needs to control and limit their workloads; and no practical way of taking into account preferences for different levels of control or independence. But although breakdowns in the relationship happened, they were relatively uncommon; students, who usually lacked a comparative framework apart from what they could glean from their peers, generally accommodated to supervision as they found it.

Both supervisors and students developed perspectives on the experience. Supervisors' perspectives were influenced by the context in which they worked, including the departmental ethos, the rewards available for different aspects of their work and ideas current in the discipline about the nature of a doctorate. Supervision should not be seen in isolation; interviews made it clear that academics were often working in conditions of considerable stress. Some of their responses to students might stem from their needs to balance commitments and pressures.

Students' perspectives were heavily influenced by where they were positioned in the enterprise. Of the three groups of home students, full-time students had made the most side-bets (Becker 1970), leaving other identities behind while immersing themselves in the research student role. Perhaps as a consequence, they were most likely to be critical of the experience. Moreover, they often had financial difficulties and were concerned about inadequate academic career opportunities. Part-time students who worked full-time on paid research projects had a different set of problems, mainly status anxiety and an inability to concentrate on the thesis. Part-time 'detached' students were the most content, although ironically they received least in the way of resources and attention from the institution. Their side-bets were elsewhere and they had less interest in academic careers. Nevertheless in some ways they were the true scholars, with a real passion for their work.

Some implications for policy

Several policy implications follow from our study. The first concerns support and training for supervisors. Supervisors learned by trial and error and rarely gained enough experience, even over a whole career, to be completely confident. Even confident ones encountered difficult students. Training materials and opportunities need to be available, although not imposed in an inflexible way that conflicts with the myriad obligations supervisors already have. Support is as important as training. Joint supervision sometimes helped, especially where it involved the pairing of an experienced with an inexperienced supervisor. The American supervisory committee model might be further explored. Such committees and pairings of supervisors help colleagues to know of the effective strategies of others. Often, insufficient recognition was given for good supervision.

Second, ESRC policy needs to recognise that students see an academic life ahead which offers uncertain prospects. They see their supervisors under stress and anxious about the impact of constantly changing government policies. Most jobs on offer are in the contract research sector. Increasing the appeal of academic life (were it possible) might improve doctoral completion rates more than many other measures as shown by Bowen and Sosa (1989 p.162) who demonstrated that in the USA a buoyant labour market, with increasing numbers of appointments and rising academic salaries, was associated with an increase in the numbers of new doctorates and a decrease in median time to completion.

Third, our findings suggest that part-time students deserve more financial help. Most of our part-time 'detached' students did not receive help from their employers; sometimes they had to circumvent barriers placed in their way. A system of bursaries to help them with fees, conference attendances and other expenses such as that recently announced by the ESRC is welcome.

Fourth, it needs to be recognised that extending training requirements and seminars seems to students to be at odds with pressure to complete more quickly. Nevertheless, such provision is necessary on other grounds. What is important is the recognition of students as heterogeneous, with ESRC-funded ones in a distinct minority. Any provision an institution makes has to take account of the diversity of actual student circumstances.

Finally, pressures for value for money should be tempered by an understanding of the creativity and time required for good research. The ESRC sanctions policy clearly resulted in improvements in submission rates, at least partly through increasing departmental and institutional consciousness of the presence of research students. Improving submission rates should not be seen as the sole purpose of research council policy, however. There is scope for bringing research students closer to full participation in academic life; students in education departments, for example, were relegated to 'student' rather than 'staff' common room space and were rarely involved in academic conferences and writing journal articles. Students and supervisors should not only be pushed towards accountability; they should be helped to experience the full rewards and pleasures of scholarship and intellectual collaboration.

References

Acker, S. (1992) New perspectives on an old problem: the position of women academics in British higher education. *Higher Education, 24*, 57–75.

Bargar, R. and Duncan, J. (1982) Cultivating creative endeavour in doctoral research. *Journal of Higher Education, 53*, 1, 1–31.

Becker, H. (1970) *Sociological Work*. New Brunswick, N.J.: Transaction Books.

Bowen, W.G. and Rudenstine, N. (1992) *In Pursuit of the PhD*. Princeton, N.J.: Princeton University Press.

Bowen, W.G. and Sosa, J.A. (1989) *Prospects for Faculty in the Arts and Science: A Study of Factors Affecting Demand and Supply, 1987 to 2012*. Princeton, N.J.: Princeton University Press.

Brown, G. and Atkins, M. (1988) *Effective Teaching in Higher Education*. London: Methuen.

Burnett Report (1977) *Report of the Vice-Chancellor's Committee on Research and Postgraduate Study*. St Lucia: University of Queensland. In I. Moses (1984) 'Supervision of Higher Degree Students – Problem Areas and Possible Solutions'. *Higher Education Research and Development, 3*, 2, 153–165.

Channell, J. (1990) The student-tutor relationship. In M. Kinnell (ed) *The Learning Experiences of Overseas Students*. Guildford: SRHE and Milton Keynes: Open University Press.

Connell, R.W. (1985) How to supervise a PhD. *Vestes 2*, 38–41.

Council of Graduate Schools (1991) *The Role and Nature of the Doctoral Dissertation*. Washington, D.C.: CGS.

Economic and Social Research Council (1991) *Postgraduate Training: Guidelines on the Provision of Research Training for Postgraduate Research Students in the Social Sciences*. Swindon: ESRC.

Friedman, N. (1987) *Mentors and Supervisors*. IIE Research Report Number 14. New York: Institute for International Education.

Kiely, M. (1982) *Creative Sensitivity in Doctoral Research: The Supervisor's Contribution*. Paper presented at the annual meeting of the American Psychological Association, Washington, D.C.

Phillips, E. and Pugh, D. (1987) *How to Get a PhD*. Milton Keynes: Open University Press.

Rudd, E. (1985) *A New Look at Postgraduate Failure*. Guildford: SRHE and Slough: NFER-Nelson.

Taylorson, D. (1984) The professional socialisation, integration and identity of women PhD candidates. In S. Acker and D. Warren Piper (eds) *Is Higher Education Fair to Women?* Guildford: SRHE and Slough: NFER-Nelson.

Welsh, J. (1982) Improving the supervision of postgraduate students. *Research in Education 27*, 1–8.

Williams, G. (1988) *Research on Research Training in the Social Sciences: Summary and Suggestions for Research Areas*. Paper prepared for the Training Board of the ESRC, London, Centre for Higher Education Studies, Institute of Education, University of London.

Winfield, G. (1987) *The Social Science PhD: The ESRC Inquiry on Submission Rates*. London: ESRC.

Wright, J. (1991) A study of the styles of PhD supervision. *Unpublished Paper*. Reading: University of Reading.

Wright, J. and Lodwick, R. (1989) The process of the PhD: a study of the first year of doctoral study. *Research Papers in Education 4*, 1 22–56.

Part II

Issues of Quality

Chapter 5

Supervisors' and Students' Experiences of Supervision

Michael Youngman

What happens in supervision?

The supervision of students carrying out research has inevitably been the focus of numerous studies and commentaries, but oddly, the opening question remains unanswered. True, we have opinions and judgements about the nature of supervision. For example, Welsh (1979) reported the subjective feelings of a small sample of students. Eggleston and Delamont (1983) collected the views of a larger group. More recently Wright (1992) has obtained reactions from students and supervisors over the full four-year span of the typical PhD research degree. And of course, the ESRC initiative reported in this volume has provided insights into many different aspects of research supervision. But a feature of the vast majority of studies to date has been a desire to interpret the relationship.

I encountered a comparable situation over twenty years ago when I joined a research team, led by John Heywood, given the task of defining training objectives for technicians and engineers. There was no shortage of advice and recommendations on training, particularly from the more expert sectors of the industry. But noticeably absent was any detailed, clear, agreed description of what the subjects of this training were actually doing in their jobs. That was not the case in the United States. There, not only could one obtain highly elaborated specifications for almost any job, but also there were groups developing analytical methods to make best use of those specifications.

Building upon that American experience our team was able to generate a strategy for analysing what actually happened in engineering jobs, and to apply the outcomes to training (Youngman, Oxtoby, Monk and Heywood 1978). So effective was the strategy that it has since been applied to very diverse occupations including secondary school teachers (Youngman 1979), nurses (Youngman, Mockett and Baxter 1988) building society branch managers (Fisher 1991) and computer science tutors (Moore 1987). Success with these situations suggested that it should be equally possible to use the approach to obtain descriptions of what actually happens in research student supervision. As with each previous application, any particular situation introduces its unique characteristics. In the case of research supervision there was the possibility of contrary perceptions to consider (a point well-documented in other studies such as McMichael 1992 and Wright 1992).

The ESRC's original brief for the research supervision initiative identified a variety of general aims. This study aimed to produce findings that would help departments, supervisors and students carry out their own tasks more effectively. To do so it sought to generate accurate and realistic descriptions of research supervision practice, and student experiences and perceptions.

A summary of the aims of the study

1. To develop a self-report instrument for describing the actual practices of research supervisors, and the experiences of research students.
2. To use this instrument to obtain detailed descriptions from a representative sample of social science research degree supervisors and students.
3. To identify similarities and differences in their accounts.
4. To suggest implications for student supervision, the evaluation of supervision, and the provision of supervisor training.

The design of the study

The general design of the study fits the conventional survey plan in most respects. The initial exploratory phase uses interviews to establish the nature of existing supervisory practice. From these interviews items are constructed, and then compiled into the main survey instrument. Responses from this instrument become the basis of subsequent analyses and conclusions. This design can be summarised as follows:

1. Select a suitable interview sample.
2. Interview to establish current practice.
3. Compile interview statements into a detailed checklist.
4. Distribute the checklist to a large, representative sample.
5. Analyse the checklists to identify research activities.

6. Examine activity variations for different groupings.

The following sections describe each stage in turn. It should be emphasised that since the study was always intended to report quickly, this inevitably led to certain limitations in design and execution. These are mentioned at appropriate points.

Select the interview sample

Information obtained from the interview sample eventually formed the main survey instrument. To ensure that the latter could cope with the anticipated variety in supervisory practice the interview sample itself had to show adequate coverage. The critical aspects to represent were role (supervisor or student), subject area, stage in the course, and possible institutional variations. The plan adopted was to conduct 20 interviews, 10 with supervisors and 10 with students, with the emphasis on completed courses. Five social science departments from three universities were considered sufficient to cover institutional range. These departments were economics, psychology, politics, social work and education. In the event there were 18 interviews since one politics student was absent and in the social work department three students were interviewed as a group. This still resulted in 10 supervisors and 10 students forming the interview base.

Interviewing to establish current practice

The aim of the interviews was to help each supervisor or student describe in detail their experience of research supervision. Supervisors were encouraged to relate their experience to several students to extend the range of tasks and tactics elicited. The students described their experiences within the course they were currently pursuing, or had recently completed. The focus of the interviews was actual practice. This slant was most easily achieved by asking interviewees to start with their first encounter, and then to proceed chronologically with their account. Any prompting that was needed was usually to emphasise the concern with actions or behaviour, rather than aims or opinions on research.

In all interviews two researchers were present. This was to maintain continuity since one did most of the talking whilst the other wrote down statements describing practice. Using this method it was possible to formulate statements that could be incorporated in the survey instrument with little or no revision. So effective was dual interviewing that even though interviews were tape recorded, these recordings were neither transcribed or replayed.

The interviews lasted from 30 to 45 minutes, generating as many as 60 items in the early stages. This number reduced as the content began to be repeated so that the final interviews produced fewer than 20 new items. This saturation supported the initial decision to restrict the study to 20 interviews. The total number of items from all the interviews was 664. The next stage was to reduce that total to a manageable size of survey instrument.

Compile the survey checklist

Item selection and specification

Previous experience of developing job analysis checklists had shown that it was possible to reduce the pilot list by between a half and two-thirds without sacrificing coverage. Consequently it seemed reasonable to try to produce a final checklist of around 300 items. The first step in this reduction process was to make a subjective classification of the items. Since the main survey analysis would ultimately generate the authentic grouping of items, all that was required at this stage was a means whereby similar or repeated items could be identified. They could then be eliminated or modified as appropriate. Several other reduction criteria were employed. Some items were made general by changing excessively specific references; certain items were considered so specific that they were removed altogether. The overall aim was to produce a checklist that was relevant to all the target sample of social science supervisors and students.

Probably the most troublesome aspect of making the checklist universally applicable was the need to accommodate supervisors and students. There are two traditional resolutions of this problem. The simplest solution is to have separate instruments for the two groups. But this may only delay the problem since ultimately the research needs to compare the experiences of supervisors and students. If the data collection instruments are different, then it follows that there must be areas where that comparison is not directly feasible. Any extrapolations across the data may become suspect. The alternative solution is to have a single checklist, but to request two (or more) responses to cover different concerns of the two groups. Usually this means offering two responses columns with either or both being ticked by the respondent. There are several drawbacks with this system. First, the task for the respondent is considerably harder. And in situations where the response levels are notoriously low any further obstacle is to be discouraged. Second, data coding is made more complex, as is any subsequent analysis of those data.

An intermediate solution was designed. The checklist statements were formulated in a manner that allowed supervisors and students to respond to the same items. Each behaviour was allied to a particular member of the team by adding the reference SUP for supervisor or STUD for student (or sometimes both). Examples:

8 SUP examines analysis results

19 STUD checks reliability of data collected

28 SUP and STUD discuss potential external examiner

This imposes two restrictions on the span of permissible items. Clearly the content must be limited to actions that both student and supervisor can be expected to know about. This meant that a good deal of the admissions procedure information had to be left out since students would not usually be party to the relevant information. But even after careful consideration of this aspect of item content it was inevitable that some uncertainty would remain, and this was made apparent in comments made by some respondents.

Effectively the adopted design of the checklist emphasises the presence of behaviour, indicated by ticking relevant boxes. The absence of a tick (i.e. 0 or blank) corresponds either to absence of the behaviour, or to no knowledge regarding the behaviour. In terms of validity, this implies that recorded levels will tend to underestimate actual levels.

The final outcome from this reduction and rewriting process was a checklist of 294 items. Their distribution across the pilot categories was as follows:

Category		*Initial N items*	*Final N items*
A	Application/Entry	68	22
B	Induction	17	10
C	Problem/Topic	26	13
D	Design/Method/Procedure	38	23
E	Analysis	50	25
F	Writing	116	54
G	Monitoring/Reporting	18	10
H	Personal	14	6
I	Funding	20	8
J	Management/Overall supervision	126	58
K	Data	40	15
L	Literature/Reading	15	7
M	Examination	91	28
N	Training	25	13
Total		**664**	**292**

Items 293 and 294 were added on the basis of personal experience.

Figure 5.1: Sample page from the research role checklist

---

61 ☐   STUD applies for research in a general area
62 ☐   SUP requests detailed project outline
63 ☐   SUP ensures applicant has ability to pursue research
64 ☐   STUD pursues topic predetermined by department
65 ☐   SUP assesses STUD personal situation before accepting
66 ☐   SUP suggests modifications following upgrading
67 ☐   STUD rejects SUP suggestions on research methods
68 ☐   SUP identifies possible error in analysis results
69 ☐   SUP suggests rephrasing of thesis sections
70 ☐   SUP provides interpretations of data/analysis
71 ☐   SUP decides on revisions needed in written material
72 ☐   STUD takes formal progress examination
73 ☐   STUD modifies initial outline as research develops
74 ☐   STUD receives written contract of tutoring duties
75 ☐   SUP supplies student with guidelines on presentation
76 ☐   STUD requests funding to present paper at conference
77 ☐   STUD reworks material to publish after completion
78 ☐   STUD and SUP meet at weekly intervals
79 ☐   STUD reorganises data into form for analysis
80 ☐   SUP encourages student to offer own ideas
81 ☐   SUP permits students to tape record meetings
82 ☐   SUP asks students to compile bibliography from start
83 ☐   STUD develops research ideas in groups of students
84 ☐   SUP tells student identity of internal examiner
85 ☐   SUP completes attendance record for meetings
86 ☐   SUP simulates viva situation for student
87 ☐   SUP briefs student on what to expect in the viva
88 ☐   STUD approaches department for tuition
89 ☐   Discuss publishable aspects of thesis in viva
90 ☐   STUD submits detailed research proposal

The Research Role Checklist was presented as an A5 booklet. The instructions for completion were followed by a single page of biographic questions. These covered role, subject area, course level, study method (full or part-time), number of research students in the department, and previous research experience. The last question needed different versions for supervisor or student. The full report contains a complete copy of the checklist.

The instructions given to respondents were slightly different from those used in the interviews. Students were again asked to describe their current or most recent course, but supervisors were asked to refer to their most recently completed research student. Whilst it was recognised that supervisors would adjust their style to match individual students, it was assumed that these variations would be accounted for across the sample of supervisors.

Checklist items were printed 30 per page, with the response box located on the left, immediately after the item number. Several respondents drew attention to this, suggesting it was a mistake. The reason for this deviation from standard practice was to maximise completion accuracy. The varying lengths of the item statements meant that most of the gaps between the ends of these statements and a right side response box would be quite long, introducing the risk of respondents scoring the wrong box. Padding out the gap with dots or lines makes the visual impression of the page too crowded. Locating the box on the left reduces the likelihood of incorrect entries being made. However it is appreciated that this format may be unfamiliar, requiring some adjustment in response style (see Figure 5.1 giving a sample page).

The checklist ended with a request for any further comments respondents might like to offer. In the event about a quarter of the sample did offer comments, many very detailed.

Distribution method

The respondent package comprised a letter outlining the purpose of the study, the checklist and a business reply service prepaid return envelope. All supervisor contacts were made via the heads of departments. Students were contacted in the same manner unless addresses had been supplied, in which case they were written to directly. The timing of this part of the study was not ideal. Delays finalising the research contract meant that these letters went out in July, leaving inadequate time for returning responses before the vacation. Indeed, some sample members did not receive their letters until the autumn term. The overall effect was to delay analysis until late October. It is also probable that having the vacation gap around the distribution time dissipated interest in the study, thereby reducing the response rate.

The main survey sample

The two major requirements of the main survey were representativeness and size. On the first count it was decided to limit attention to England and Scotland, since speed was becoming important. As regards size, several considerations were involved. The eventual sample had to be large enough for the anticipated analyses, so some estimate of response rate was needed. In previous applications of the method (using longer checklists) rates of between 40 per cent (for school teachers) and 64 per cent (for hospital nurses and technicians) had been achieved. It seemed reasonable to expect a response of around 50 per cent bearing in mind the closeness of the topic to the interests of the proposed sample.

Assuming that 200 cases would be needed to permit effective subgroup and multivariate analysis, a contact sample of around 400 was decided upon. Allowing for non-participation it was felt that contacting 30 departments should meet the requirements of size and representation. Consequently five departments from each of six universities were selected as the contact sample. The departments were chosen to cover social science disciplines; the universities were selected on the basis of having a particular initial letter in their name. None of the pilot universities were included.

Table 5.1 summarises the distribution, participation and response rate characteristics of the sample. Clearly the 25 per cent response rate achieved fell well short of the planning estimate of 50 per cent. Some adjustments to the rate should be made to allow for checklists returned through address changes, or from academic staff not involved in supervision. It is also known that at least one batch of letters was not sent out by the department. It is almost certain that the standard quantities supplied to departments which did not specify precise requirements were optimistic estimates of numbers. These various adjustments probably raise the effective response rate to between 30 and 40 per cent. The effect of the vacation timing has also been mentioned, but it cannot be quantified. Disappointment has to be expressed when so many supervisors and students felt unable to participate in the first national survey of an activity so close to their concerns.

Table 5.1: Contact, participation and response samples details

Univ Department	Participate		Number Sent		Number Retrnd	
	No	Yes	SUP	STUD	SUP	STUD
1 Anthropology	NO					
1 Economics	N/R					
1 Geography	NO					
1 Laws	N/R					
1 Psychology		YES	30	10	4	4
2 Economics	N/R					
2 Education		YES	17	30	5	9
2 Marketing		YES	12	12	3	2
2 Politics	N/R					
2 Psychology		YES	20	20	1	4
3 Continuing Education		YES	5	10	2	5
3 Economics	N/R					
3 Geography		YES	20	20	2	4
3 Management	N/R					
3 Social Policy	N/R					
4 Continuing Education	N/R					
4 Economics		YES	3	4	3	2
4 Politics	N/R					
4 Psychology	N/R					
4 Sociology		YES	23	23	4	2
5 Geography		YES	15	15	4	3
5 Politics	NO					
5 Psychology		YES	18	25	4	7
5 Social Policy		YES	10	23	3	6
5 Sociology	NO					
6 Education	NO					
6 Geography		YES	6	15	4	9
6 Politics		YES	12	15	2	0
6 Psychology		YES	5	10	4	2
6 Sociology	N/R					2
Totals	**16**	**14**	**196**	**232**	**45**	**61**
			428		106 =	25%

The actual numbers responding (45 supervisors and 61 students) must also restrict the scope of subsequent analyses. However, the critical analysis, clustering to identify activity patterns, remains practicable even though its reliability is reduced. Similarly the roughly equal split between supervisors and students preserves the ability to conduct some comparison of roles.

There are positive features in the sample that should not be overlooked. All six universities are represented with 14 departments providing responses. Of the 28 departmental subgroups only two supply fewer than two responses. Typically there are four to six responses per group which should cover the sort of variation one might expect both within departments and between them. And finally this is the time to reiterate the earlier comment regarding the exploratory nature of this particular study, with its objective of generating early insights to be incorporated in other larger studies within the supervision initiative.

General response patterns from the survey

The analyses of the survey responses fall into two main areas. Firstly there are the general patterns describing the response sample itself, and the overall checklist findings. Following these an activity structure is generated to enable a more coherent account of the response tendencies to be developed. There is a discussion of the first analysis area followed by the activity analyses.

Characteristics of the response sample

The broad picture of the response sample as shown in Table 5.1 can be refined using information from the biographic page of the checklist. Table 5.2 summarises this information. Since the total sample for this part is 106 cases (i.e. approximately 100) it is not considered necessary to report percentage results as well as actual numbers since the two would be virtually identical.

General observations from the sample data are as follows:

(b) **Subject area** The bulk of the sample falls into the four subject areas education, geography, psychology or social studies.

(c) **Course** There is a clear bias towards doctorate level study.

Table 5.2: Characteristics of the sample (N=106)

(a) Role	N	(b) Subject area	N
1 Supervisor	45	1 Anthropology	6
2 Student	61	2 Economics	5
		3 Education	20
		4 Geography	26
(c) Course	N	5 Management	0
1 Master's	19	6 Marketing	6
2 Doctorate	86	7 Politics	3
N/R	1	8 Psychology	30
		9 Social/S Wrk	9
		N/R	1
(d) Study method	N		
1 Part-time	24	(e) Research students	N
2 Part + full	23	1 under 5	58
3 Full time	59	2 5–20	56
		3 21–50	27
		4 over 50	3
(f) Student experience	(N= 61)	N/R	12
1 None	7		
2 Bachelors	29		
3 Master's	24		
N/R	1		

(g) Supervisor experience   (N =45)

Current	Master's	PhDs	Completed	Master's	PhDs
None	26	8	None	20	7
1	12	19	1	15	17
2	3	4	2	2	5
3	1	7	3	5	5
4	2	3	4		4
5	1	3	5		
6			6	1	3
7		1	7		1
			8	1	1
			9		
			10	1	2

(d) **Study method** Although the majority of courses are full-time, there are sufficient part-time students to enable useful comparisons to be made between the two modes of study.

(e) **Research students** The typical size is between 5 and 20 but a quarter of the sample are from larger departments (21 to 50).

(f) **Student experience** Very few have no prior training in research but the remainder split roughly equally into those with bachelor's level experience and those with master's level.

(g) **Supervisor experience** The tendency is towards doctorate level supervision with the numbers involved relatively small. Fewer than half the sample have more than one current PhD student, and the same applies to completed PhDs. Only seven supervisors (15%) have supervised to completion more than four PhDs. The maximum number recorded is ten.

Checklist response patterns

Whilst the 294 statements in the checklist do provide a valuable base for description of supervisory practice, the prime function of the statements is to generate a structure of research activities. In order to condense the reporting of the checklist data, most of it will be related to the activity structure. Here only a summary of the responses will be offered. Anyone seeking response frequencies for individual checklist statements can obtain them from Appendix 1 and Appendix 2 of the main report (Youngman 1989).

A major theme of this study is to compare the supervisory experiences of supervisors and students. To assist that a simple classification of items has been developed. Firstly response levels are categorised in relation to percentages of supervisors or students responding. A 50 per cent response is taken as the criterion for high or low levels. Accordingly we have:

B = Both (supervisors and students) exceed 50 per cent

T = Tutors (supervisors) only exceed 50 per cent

S = Students only exceed 50 per cent

N = Neither group exceeds 50 per cent

The second feature of the classification of items is a test of the significance of the difference in the response levels of the two analysis groups. A conventional chi-square test is applied to the 2 x 2 table formed by totalling the numbers of YES or NO responses for the supervisors and students. Labelling is as follows:

+ = Students respond significantly higher than supervisors
- = Students respond significantly lower than supervisors
Blank = There is no significant difference

Category		No of Items		n +	n -
B	Both high	82 ⌐		+	-
B+	Both high STUD higher	2	107	2+	-
B-	Both high STUD lower	23 ⌐		+	23-
S+	STUD high and significant	6 ⌐		6+	-
S	STUD high	6		+	-
T	SUP high	13	63	+	-
T-	SUP high STUD lower	38 ⌐		+	38-
N	Both low	112 ⌐		+	-
N+	Both low STUD higher	0	124	+	-
N-	Both low STUD lower	12 ⌐		+	12-
	Totals	**294**		**8+**	**73-**

This produces 10 different combinations of the two labels (not 12 since T+ and S- are logically impossible). When all 294 items are categorised under this system the tabulated distribution results. It shows that just over a third of the items register a high response level overall. About a fifth produce intermediate levels. Two-fifths (124 items) have response levels below 50 per cent. These figures can be taken to indicate good discrimination across the checklist. Further evidence of discrimination appears in the supervisor/student significance testing summarised in the right-hand columns. The tests show over a quarter of the items (81) recording significantly different response levels. In the vast majority of these instances (73) the supervisors score higher.

Clearly general summaries of this kind need considerable elaboration before formative conclusions can be drawn. At this stage there are two main findings of note. Certainly the response variability augurs well for subsequent analyses. A second finding relates to the response differences. Even without listing all the 81 items involved it is possible to see major factors operating. The list below shows the first 6 checklist items for which the difference between the supervisor and student response levels is greater than 30 per cent. In all cases this difference is highly significant (p<.01); indeed as a rule of thumb any difference of 20 per cent is significant (p<.05) whilst a difference of 30 per cent achieves the .01 level.

Item	*SUP%*	*STUD%*	
4	80	48	SUP tightens initial outline proposal from STUD
6	9	52	STUD makes own decisions on all procedures
13	93	62	SUP approves submission of final thesis draft
23	96	64	SUP directs STUD towards start points in literature
25	80	43	SUP informs STUD of name of external examiner
30	76	41	STUD is informed of outcome at end of viva

The last three items all refer to tasks associated with the final stages of the research. It is apparent from these and many other similar items that a substantial proportion of the research students in the sample are still on course. The three items listed here suggest that the proportion is around 30 per cent but not more than 35 per cent (item 30). If it is assumed that most supervisors have, as requested, described their most recently completed student, then later analyses need to be interpreted accordingly.

The other three items listed here seem to raise issues of a more fundamental nature. Item 6 is especially revealing, suggesting an intrinsically different perspective on the supervision process. Items 4 and 23 add support to this initial interpretation of findings. Any further development of these interpretations will be based on the activity analyses presented in the next section.

Ten supervision activities

Identification of the activities

The expansive checklist of supervision experience guarantees high validity through its good coverage of the domain, but normally this would be bought at the expense of efficient analysis. This risk is overcome by developing an integral method which capitalises on the breadth of the database. The analytical component of the method uses cluster analysis to identify intrinsic groupings of the checklist items. In some respects this is similar to factoring variables into underlying dimensions. The differences are that considerably more variables (items) can be incorporated, and the subsequent interpretation is more direct. The analytical details are not presented here but Youngman (1978 1979) provides information on the job analysis strategy and the particular classification method used. The centroid relocation method is selected because of its capability with large datasets and large samples, and because of its proven ability to generate replicable and interpretable classifications. Interpretability is one of the strengths of clustering over factoring through the production of disjoint groups of items. The items forming each cluster can be listed, allowing the nature of the group to be readily seen. A name or label can be allocated to simplify later analyses using the clusters.

In the same way that in factor analysis there is an element of subjectivity in the choice of the number of factors present, in cluster analysis a comparable decision has to be made regarding the number of clusters. The final solution will balance a mixture of statistical and interpretational criteria. Minimising error means that clusters are relatively homogenous whilst maintaining good discrimination between clusters. Discrimination is further assisted by having enough clusters to go beyond the grosser variations in response characteristics, and typically this requires from 5 to 20 clusters. And of course the research issue can only be served by identifying groups that are interpretable.

Applying these considerations led to a choice of 10 clusters. These were nine clusters from the 10-cluster array with the addition of a cluster concerned with analysis which arose during a preliminary clustering of the data. The cluster eliminated was considered trivial since it comprised only four items (27, 58, 112 and 140) and the last two of them were identical. These clusters of items are referred to as ACTIVITIES to reflect their behavioural nature, and because their analytical proximity arises from the fact that grouped items tend to occur together in the reported experiences of respondents. Each activity is given a name to simplify later references to it. The 10 activities are as follows:

The number of constituent items varies from 8 to 44 but even the smallest have enough items for scores derived from the activities to meet psychometric criteria. In fact reliabilities based on clustered scales are invariably high. Here all values exceed 0.7.

The following summary lists the eight most central items for each activity. Centrality is given by the item-activity correlation. The percentages of supervisors and students ticking the items are listed with significant differences indicated (*p<.05, **p<.01). with several around 0.9. Activities 3 RARE OCCURRENCES and 4 COLLABORATION register the lowest reliabilities. Their average usage levels are also low. This statistic gives the averaged proportion of the sample ticking the items making up the activity. So on average only 7 per cent of the sample respond to the items forming activity 3, and indeed it is more a statistical artefact than a recognisable activity. The label RARE OCCURRENCES signals this. At 21 per cent usage activity 4 has the next lowest recorded usage so again some consideration of that may be needed in discussing later analyses.

		No. of items	Average Usage	Alpha
1	Thesis guidance	19	.75	.89
2	Design guidance	10	.67	.83
3	Rare occurrence	41	.07	.73
4	Collaboration	39	.21	.75
5	Student direction	44	.80	.91
6	Submission guidance	11	.62	.87
7	Student studying	15	.45	.87
8	Supervisor control	15	.25	.77
9	Analysis guidance	8	.44	.76
10	Student control	12	.68	.86
	All Activities	**214**	**.33**	**.86**
	All Checklist	**294**	**.33**	**.91**

A fuller picture of the activities can be obtained from the complete listing of the items comprising each activity. These are given in Appendix 1 of the report (Youngman 1989). What follows is an outline in sufficient detail for the main analyses to be readily comprehended. The Inset summarises each activity.

Inset

ACTIVITY 1 Thesis guidance (19 items)

Item	Cent	SUP%	STUD%	
157	.69	89	** 54	SUP provides guidance on thesis drafting
98	.65	96	** 64	SUP advises student on style and presentation
183	.62	87	** 56	SUP informs STUD of thesis format requirements
69	.60	93	** 59	SUP suggests rephrasing of thesis sections
146	.60	89	** 51	SUP informs student of procedural requirements
283	.60	91	77	SUP inspects all draft thesis chapters
102	.54	82	* 59	SUP suggests modifications to initial thesis outline
273	.53	82	* 62	SUP makes written comments on STUD's analysis

ACTIVITY 2 Design guidance (10 items)

Item	Cent	SUP%	STUD%	
8	.64	91	** 67	SUP examines analysis results
178	.61	76	59	SUP advises on suitability of analysis methods
99	.60	87	** 52	SUP confirms interpretation of data/analysis
189	.54	84	69	SUP directs STUD towards suitable sources
243	.54	87	** 62	SUP and STUD discuss evaluation of statistical data
49	.53	78	** 41	SUP examines raw data
96	.50	76	* 52	SUP vets draft research instrument
4	.43	80	** 48	SUP tightens initial outline proposal from STUD

ACTIVITY 3 Rare occurrences (41 items)

Item	Cent	SUP	STUD%	
254	.62	9	2	SUP seeks help for STUD needing extra help to pass
143	.50	11	10	SUP gives guidelines on correction of failed thesis
174	.49	2	0	SUP advises STUD to transfer to other institution
192	.46	7	2	STUD expresses concern over nominated examiner
35	.45	7	7	SUP discourages candidate from starting
251	.40	27	** 7	SUP explains supervisor's role change on submission
81	.39	13	7	SUP permits student to tape record meetings
250	.34	13	3	SUP chastises STUD for showing lack of effort

ACTIVITY 4 Collaboration (39 items)

Item	Cent	SUP%	STUD%	
234	.47	31	23	STUD consults one SUP on advice from another
103	.43	18	25	STUD consults SUP to overcome personal problems
142	.42	20	10	SUP advises against submission of weak thesis
236	.42	13	15	SUP informs referred candidate of extra work needed
275	.42	16	11	SUP negotiates with sample over problem
264	.40	27	11	SUP contacts sources for specialist advice
40	.36	40	** 10	SUP requires STUD to obtain analysis training
88	.35	16	18	STUD approaches department for tuition

ACTIVITY 5 Student direction (44 items)

Item	Cent	SUP%	STUD%	
240	.62	78	89	STUD investigates materials for research procedure
53	.59	89	89	STUD examines literature to develop initial outline

124	.58	71	74	STUD prepares research instrument
138	.58	71	* 89	STUD identifies theory behind literature review
271	.56	80	82	STUD selects appropriate data analysis method
34	.55	80	84	STUD identifies theory pertinent to the research
148	.55	78	84	STUD compares obtained data with theory
38	.53	78	89	STUD judges reliabilty/validity of analyses

ACTIVITY 6 Submission guidance (11 items)

Item Cent SUP%STUD%

114	.70	87	** 64	SUP satisfies self that thesis is likely to pass
13	.69	93	** 62	SUP approves submission of final thesis draft
194	.65	84	** 43	SUP informs STUD of time and location of viva
227	.59	76	** 36	STUD and SUP meet after graduation
84	.58	84	** 46	SUP tells STUD identity of external examiner
87	.57	78	** 39	SUP briefs STUD on what to expect in viva
126	.56	76	** 44	SUP comments to STUD on final typed thesis
30	.53	76	** 41	STUD is informed of outcome at end of viva

ACTIVITY 7 Student studying (15 items)

Item Cent SUP%STUD%

46	.66	58	61	STUD receives assistance to attend conference
16	.65	58	54	STUD requests assistance to attend conference
76	.61	42	36	STUD requests funding to give paper at conference
171	.60	51	33	STUD learns computing from formal course
186	.53	56	54	STUD presents paper to major conference
241	.53	51	* 30	STUD receives formal tuition in computing
244	.52	53	26	SUP offers help with journal paper
242	.51	49	34	STUD prepares paper on research for circulation

ACTIVITY 8 Supervisor control (15 items)

Item Cent SUP%STUD%

226	.57	36	* 15	SUP requires STUD to learn word processing skills
162	.53	31	* 11	SUP demonstrates desirable behaviour in the field
78	.52	36	20	STUD and SUP meet at weekly intervals
135	.47	29	16	SUP observes STUD operating in the field
281	.43	22	25	STUD receives formal tuition in word processing
108	.41	47	** 15	SUP provides extensive direction
136	.38	47	28	SUP demands regular attendance
218	.36	40	23	STUD and SUP discuss another student's methodology

ACTIVITY 9 Technical guidance (8 items)

Item	Cent	SUP%	STUD%	
110	.63	80	** 26	SUP augments bibliography supplied by student
196	.48	60	** 21	SUP identifies suitable courses inside department
248	.46	60	39	SUP identifies sources of specialist advice
255	.46	69	** 41	SUP directs STUD towards texts on research methods
239	.44	71	** 41	SUP identifies broad conceptual framework of topic
258	.43	51	** 25	STUD receives formal tuition in data analysis
68	.39	56	** 16	SUP identifies possible error in analysis results
70	.36	62	** 30	SUP provides interpretation of data/analysis

ACTIVITY 10 Student control (12 items)

Item	Cent	SUP%	STUD%	
154	.70	71	62	STUD learns to prepare data for computer analysis
127	.69	76	64	STUD learns how to access mainframe computer
249	.68	69	62	STUD prepares data for input to computer
265	.61	71	57	STUD enters data into computer
204	.57	76	72	STUD consults other staff in Department for help
156	.52	71	70	STUD offers seminar on research
182	.52	82	72	STUD attends research student seminars
231	.50	69	69	STUD codes data

An outline of the ten activities

From the names listed above there do appear to be three groups of activities. The four guidance activities (1, 2, 6 and 9) cover four well-recognised aspects of research. Three others (5, 7 and 10) identify student-orientated behaviour. That leaves three activities and, as might be expected, they lean towards supervisor involvement.

Any further interpretation of the relationships between the activities is best carried out on a statistical basis. To do this it is first necessary to use the psychometric properties of the activities. In particular the high alpha coefficients justify adding an individual's responses to the items forming an activity to produce a composite score on that activity. This is then converted to a percentage to counter the varying number of items per activity. These activity usage scores can be analysed using the full repertoire of statistical procedures. Table 5.3 shows the intercorrelation matrix derived from the activity scores.

Table 5.3: Intercorrelation matrix for the ten activities

Activity	1	2	3	4	5	6	7	8	9
1 Thesis guidance									
2 Design guidance	60								
3 Rare occurrence	43	40							
4 Collaboration	19	23	51						
5 Student direction	25	20	14	18					
6 Submission guidance	67	44	37	02	29				
7 Student studying	34	17	26	26	41	38			
8 Supervisor control	40	40	38	32	14	30	41		
9 Analysis guidance	51	51	37	34	09	33	34	52	
10 Student control	19	27	13	27	62	26	63	28	30

In general it confirms the apparent grouping already described. The links between the guidance activities are particularly strong, as are those for the student activities. The least well-defined set consists of the three supervisors' activities, supporting the reservations already expressed over the low incidence activities, 3 and 4. One valuable feature of the correlations is the relative independence of the student activities, most clearly seen in the row of correlations for 10, STU-DENT CONTROL. This is likely to be helpful in identifying differences in perceptions of supervisors and students. Conversely the SUPERVISOR CONTROL activity (8) shows moderately high correlations with the supervisor and the guidance activities, indicating that, as one might expect, these guidance activities are orientated towards supervisor behaviour.

Patterns of involvement within the sample

Overall involvement

The activity summary given above includes an average usage statistic. For the complete checklist of 294 items the average usage level is .33, indicating that a typical respondent ticks one third of the items. But global statistics are of limited value. More information is gained from the variations in response patterns across the activities. The peculiar nature of activity 3, RARE OCCURRENCES, with its very low usage score of only 5 per cent has already been explained as more a statistical feature than an identifiable activity. For the remaining activities, however, usage levels range from .11 to .80, indicating that

Table 5.4: Group average activity scores

Grouping	Group Size N	ThG 1	DeG 2	Rar 3	Col 4	StD 5	SbG 6	StS 7	SuC 8	AnG 9	StC 10	Tot
Role												
1 Supervisor	45	90+	81+	10+	22	77	80+	51	34+	64+	70	36+
		■	■	■			■		■	■		■
2 Student	61	63-	56-	05-	20	82	48-	40	19-	30-	66	30-
Course												
1 Master's	19	68	69	05	19	72-	44-	22-	15-	43	53-	28-
						■	■	■	■		■	■
2 PhD	86	77	67	08	22	82+	66+	50+	28+	45	71+	34+
Study Method												
1 Part-time	24	70	67	06	19	73	55	21-	19	41	48-	28-
								■	■	■	■	■
2 Part + Full	23	66	62	08	26	83	53	39	16-	28-	72	32
								■	■	■	■	■
3 Full-time	59	79	69	08	20	81	67	56+	32+	52+	74+	35+
Student Experience												
1 None	7	46	60	05	17	76	44	16-	05	16	45	24-
								■			■	■
2 Bachelors	29	67	51	05	21	83	48	55+	23	33	74+	32
								■			■	■
3 Master's	24	64	60	05	20	82	47	30	17	29	61	29
Supervisor Experience												
1 No past PhDs	7	82	71	03	16	61	58-	21-	19	55	39-	27-
							■	■			■	■
2 1 or 2 PhDs	22	90	83	13	27	77	81	58	34	67	73	38
							■	■			■	■
3 3 or more	16	93	83	09	19	84	88	53	40	62	80	38

Notes: a Scores entered are activity averages converted to percentages.
b Significant one-way ANOVA results are indicated by a ■.
Significance markers + or - indicate whether that group scores significantly higher or lower than the remaining groups in the classification, using the appropriate Scheffe test (p<.05).
c Full activity names are given in the Section on the identification of activities

more likely reflect actual behaviour patterns. The most prominent activities are orientated towards the product of the course (THESIS GUIDANCE, SUBMISSION GUIDANCE and DESIGN GUIDANCE) or they suggest a student dominated relationship (STUDENT DIRECTION and STUDENT CONTROL). In all these cases usage levels exceed 60 per cent. At the other extreme neither COLLABORATION nor SUPERVISOR CONTROL scores over 25 per cent, corroborating the overall pattern of student domination.

Activity patterns related to individual characteristics

The biographic data were collected so that variations related to the particular circumstances of the respondents could be examined. The main features included were role, subject area, course, study method, departmental size and previous research experience. Differences were identified by subdividing the sample on the basis of these variables, and then conducting one-way analyses of variance followed by the appropriate group comparisons test (t-test for two groups, Tukey test for three or more). Table 5.4 shows the results of these analyses. Because of the sparseness of the supervisor experience categories they were conflated into three groups of no students, one or two students, or more than two students. No significant differences were found for the subject area, departmental size or three of the supervisor experience subgroupings. For the other categories descriptions employing graphical profiles follow.

Role differences

In normal circumstances the differing perceptions and experiences of supervisors and students would provide important pointers to possible developments in supervisory arrangements. Unfortunately, as has already been mentioned in some detail, in this particular sample it cannot be assumed that differences in activity profiles stem solely from contrary experiences. There is evidence to suggest that about 30 per cent of the student sample are partway through their courses, leading inevitably to lower scores on activities associated with later stages of research study. Figure 5.2, which compares the activity profiles of supervisors and students, does reflect that phenomenon to some extent with three of the six significant differences occurring in late activities (1, 6 and 9).

But there are also differences in activities that would not necessarily be associated with the final stages. The higher scores of supervisors on DESIGN GUIDANCE, ANALYSIS GUIDANCE and SUPERVISOR CONTROL would support the interpretation that su-

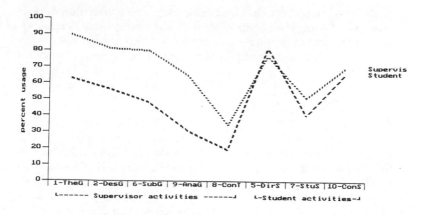

Figure 5.2: Activity profiles by role

pervisors see themselves as more directive than is the view of these students. If this can be corroborated in other analyses, then clearly it has important implications for practice.

Course level

A surprisingly small proportion of the response sample were studying at master's level (18%) rendering conclusions here rather speculative. There is an apparent tendency for greater student control (Figure 5.3, activities 5, 7 and 10) by PhD students but this seems to be contradicted somewhat by their higher score on 8, SUPERVISOR

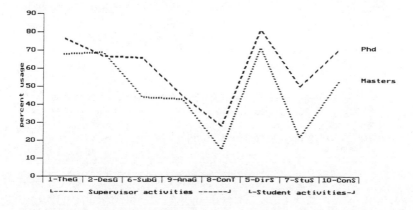

Figure 5.3: Activity profiles by course

CONTROL. However the activity listings show that the student control and supervisor control items need not be mutually exclusive. An appropriate interpretation might be that PhD students engender more involvement from supervisors through their own greater involvement.

Method of study

Although the majority of the students described were following full-time courses, almost half reported some part-time study. The general tendency shown in Figure 5.4 is similar to that described for the course groupings, with the full-time students matching the PhD profile. In some areas the differences between the part-time and full-time students are quite considerable. STUDENT STUDYING and STUDENT CONTROL are the most prominent, indicating a lower level of involvement for part-time students. Since there is not a correspondingly greater supervisor direction, it would seem that the traditional view of part-time study being rather isolated does hold. One small detail that may be worth further study is the switch in status between full-time and part-time study. The longer courses of social science students make this switch more likely. The lower levels on activities 8 and 9 for students experiencing both modes of study may point to some difficulty in making the transition. And since the change usually occurs towards the end of the course, completion rates may be affected.

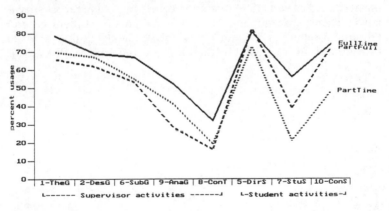

Figure 5.4: Activity profiles by method

Student research experience

The level of experience ranges from none to master's, but only seven fall into the lowest category. With the rest splitting almost equally (29 bachelor's, 24 master's) the amount of variation in reported practice is rather less than might have been expected. Even the areas of difference do not reflect a simple expertise effect. Students with only bachelor's level preparation do show a greater involvement in STUDENT STUDYING (Figure 5.5) but they also score higher on SUPERVISOR CONTROL and STUDENT CONTROL. The overall picture is really one of a more participative role for the less experienced students. It would be unwise to pursue this too far since there are likely to be other factors such as age and subject area which could explain these differences. Certainly it is not justifiable to make the simple assumption that prior study automatically fits a student for independent, self-directed research behaviour. More likely it is the specificity of research training that matters, a point of view that has emerged in the background research on training and supervision.

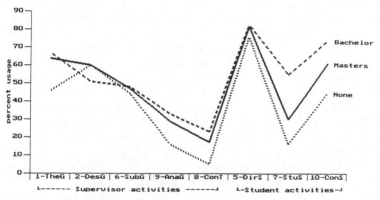

Figure 5.5: Role profiles by student experience

Supervisor research experience

Supervisor experience was measured in terms of current and completed supervision of master's and PhD students, but the only category that registered significant differences in response was completed doctorates. Figure 5.6 charts these results. With so few supervisors responding the three groups are relatively small (7, 22 and 16) respectively) but the consistency of the pattern is probably

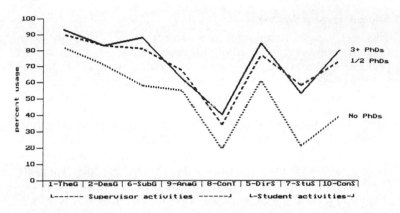

Figure 5.6: Activity profiles by supervisor experience

indicative of a broader tendency. For example, STUDENT CONTROL and STUDENT DIRECTION increase as the supervisor's experience increases. The associated increase in SUPERVISOR CONTROL corresponds with comments above regarding the more participative style that seems to go with greater student orientation. There is a further hint of this in the apparent but non-significant trends in three of the four guidance activities. It is interesting to note that supervisors are the only category where the RARE OCCURRENCES activity exceeds 10 per cent, reaching 13 per cent for the intermediate group. This suggests that in later analyses (especially clustering of respondents) these items may take on a discriminatory function in identifying idiosyncratic supervisory styles.

That completes the systematic presentation of the quantitative analyses derived from the checklist responses. A proportion of the respondents (approximately 20%) took up the invitation to comment further at the end of the checklist. These comments tended either to provide accounts (sometimes very detailed) of their personal experiences of research, or to criticise aspects of the research design, usually the checklist. Comments on the checklist centred on its length, tediousness, difficulty in completion, ambiguity of certain items, irrelevance to their situation, or positioning of boxes (already explained). Without wanting to dismiss such comments, it is suggested that some of this disapproval may be subject specific. The same format (but invariably with longer checklists) has been used in so many different work arenas for justifiable confidence in the method. What may be unique in the present study is the extent to which highly personal perceptions and decisions determine the nature of the course. This in turn would support any development of this preparatory study taking a more interactive approach. At the moment, though, the findings themselves do seem to have generated the kinds of initial insight sought of this small-scale survey.

Summary and conclusions

Even allowing for the smallness of the survey samples the conclusions emerging do confirm some of the suggestions arising from earlier studies, but at the same time they provide additional insights. From the breadth of the sample it has been argued that the sample is likely to have representative value. This is supported by a recent survey of management research students (Buckley and Hooley 1988) which achieved a supervisor sample of the same size (N=45). They also reported supervisory loads and experience, resulting in distributions virtually identical to those shown in Table 5.2. Both studies highlight the very limited supervision experience present in social science departments with only a third of supervisors having more than two completed Phd supervisions. Moreover this does appear to be a significant factor in the nature of the supervision students receive. Figure 5.6 (supervisor experience) clearly shows the lower level of involvement of supervisors and students for those supervisors who have not completed doctoral level experience. On the other hand the more experienced supervisors engender a higher level of independence from their students, whilst at the same time maintaining the high guidance profile likely to be associated with success.

The training aspects of research study were investigated by a variety of checklist items, which were later related to situational factors in general (e.g. subject, course level) and to more direct factors (departmental size and previous training). Analysis of the checklist structure identified one activity directly concerned with STUDENT STUDYING, and four others covering the guidance associated with different stages of research. The students' courses are influential in the sense that full-time students and PhD students show substantially higher levels of involvement in the STUDENT STUDYING activity. Differences in guidance levels are restricted to more ANALYSIS GUIDANCE for full-time students, and more SUBMISSION GUIDANCE for PhD students. Experience also tends to affect study levels. Students with bachelor's level backgrounds show more involvement in STUDENT STUDYING than either of the other two categories (none or master's). The effect of supervisor experience is less clear since only the small group with no completed PhDs is different, having a lower score. The actual score levels on STUDENT STUDYING are also worth noting since they range from an average of 22 per cent for the part-time students to 57 per cent for full-timers. Overall the picture here is not quite so unsatisfactory as some suggest. It is probably the variable occurrence of the study activity that needs attention. It cannot be desirable for part-time students to be further penalised by reduced access to study and guidance facilities.

Another feature of Buckley and Hooley's (1988) study that is replicated here is the strong degree of student autonomy in social science research. They reported half their sample choosing their research topics. Here the STUDENT DIRECTION activity identifies 44 items for which the average response level is 80 per cent. Probably the clearest indication of student orientation is seen in item 80:SUP encourages STUD to offer own ideas. Responses are 100 per cent and 92 per cent respectively for supervisors and students. The remaining items in this activity define a broad area within which response levels range consistently between 70 per cent and 95 per cent.

An interesting qualification to the general picture of student centred study is the extent to which supervisors and students agree on that perception. Certainly if attention is restricted to individual items it is possible to point to clear disagreements. So for example on item 108: SUP provides extensive direction, 47 per cent of supervisors say YES to the item, but only 15 per cent of students do. Perceptions are clearly different. But attitudinal analyses at item level are notoriously unreliable. When the more reliable scale or activity level analyses are examined the picture is much more consistent and interpretable. As the role profiles show, significant differences are restricted to certain guidance activities, and these almost certainly derive from the presence of on-course students in the sample rather than an intrinsic perceptual discrepancy between supervisors and students.

Applications and developments

The findings provide several indications for developments in practice. On the training side there is a need for a better coverage in provision to ensure that all students have equal access to its benefits. There is a further suggestion that the content of this training may need to be more specific to the topics and strategies of individual students. There is little evidence to suggest that generalist components in undergraduate or master's courses are in themselves adequate. As regards supervision the experience factor does seem important. Ways of introducing that include such arrangements as group supervision and supervisor training. It would be foolish to disregard the strongly student-centred nature of social science research. As Buckley and Hooley (1988) point out, this produces powerful commitment from the student. But equally it introduces the risks of slower completion and poorer success rates. One observation on supervision that is not supported here concerns supervisor's loads. With only one supervisor having more than five current research students in total, it is unlikely that overloading is a widespread problem in the social sciences.

Alongside the substantive benefits of the findings the methodology itself has considerable applied value. It would be a straightforward task to extend the checklist to accommodate the more specialised practices of other disciplines. Given that much of the discussion in this area is related to subject differences, the checklist would enable this discussion to be given an empirical base that is currently lacking (see Cox's, 1988, references to Schon's work in Annexe B of the Winfield Report 1987). Even in its existing form the checklist could be used as a basis for monitoring or evaluating present practice. However there is probably more to be gained from the structure provided by the 10 research activities. The inherent coherence of the items comprising each activity means that a sample of the items (10 or even fewer) could be used without sacrificing much of the discriminatory power of the reduced checklist. Even the activity names can be used as descriptors for quick ratings of research when allied to such constructs as incidence, importance or desirability.

Switching to the other side of the relationship, a good deal of comment is now being offered on the importance of supervisor training. But a problem in that area is the identification of suitable content. Too often anecdotal and personal recollection is used to determine training needs. The checklist and activity structure could break that introspective circle. Suitable areas for training could be identified by supervisors or students at whatever level of detail was thought appropriate. Ratings of activities or completion of the whole checklist could lead directly to training content.

It would be remiss not to draw attention to the apparent shortcomings of the study. The low response and some of the additional comments offered by respondents make it clear that many supervisors and students prefer to describe their experiences in a more interactive manner. This effectively requires visits, interviews, meetings, discussions and of course observation. It is hoped to be able to develop this particular study along those lines. Some of the other studies in the current initiative already fulfil those needs.

Acknowledgement

The research team would like to express its sincere thanks to all the students and supervisors who gave generously of their time in responding to our requests for information. We are also grateful to the ESRC for their grant in support of this work.

References

Buckley, P.J. and Hooley, G.J. (1988) The non-completion of doctoral research in management. *Educational Research 30*, 110–120.

Cox, R. (1988) *Postgraduate Research Training: Reviews of Literature and Data Sources. The Characteristics of the Training Process and Those Undergoing Research Training.* London: Institute of Education.

Eggleston, J.F. and Delamont, S. (1983) *Supervision of Students for Research Degrees with Special Reference to Educational Studies.* Birmingham: British Educational Research Association.

Fisher, K. (1991) What's in a job: Implications for structuring and accrediting work-related learning. *Unpublished PhD Thesis,* University of Lancaster.

McMichael, P. (1992) Tales of the unexpected: Supervisors and students' perspectives on short-term projects and dissertations. *Educational Studies 18,* 299–310.

Moore, J.L. (1987) The identification of teacher-style in computer studies: an analysis of teacher activities. *Educational Studies 13,* 203–212.

Welsh, J.M. (1979) *The First Year of Postgraduate Study.* Guildford, Surrey: The Society for Research into Higher Education.

Winfield, G. (1987) The Social Science PhD: The ESRC Inquiry on Submission Rates. (The Winfield Papers). London: ESRC.

Wright, J. (1992) Selection, supervision and the academic management of research leading to the degree of Phd. *Unpublished PhD Thesis,* University of Nottingham.

Youngman, M.B. (1979) *Analysing Teachers Activities: Final Report.* London: Social Science Research Council.

Youngman, M.B. (1989) *Role Expectations of Research Supervisors and Students.* Final Report R231786. Swindon: Economic and Social Research Council.

Youngman, M.B., Mockett, S. and Baxter, C. (1988) *The Intrinsic Roles of Nurses and Technicians in High Technology Clinical Areas.* London: DHSS.

Youngman, M.B., Oxtoby, R., Monk, J.D. and Heywood, J. (1978) *Analysing Jobs.* Farnborough: Gower Press.

Chapter 6

The Development of Writing Skills in Doctoral Research Students

Mark S. Torrance and Glyn V. Thomas

The ability to produce clear and concise writing efficiently is required in almost every kind of scientific or professional employment. Clear writing, indeed, is rated as more important in many jobs taken by social science graduates than good intellectual capacity, social skills or competence in handling numbers (see Chapter 10). Adequate writing ability is, of course, also required for successful completion of a doctoral thesis, which in the UK is the main product of research training to be examined. Although clear writing is a skill many find difficult, relatively little attention has been given to systematic instruction in high level writing for postgraduate students. In this chapter we will first examine the extent of writing-related difficulties encountered by research students. We will then consider the role and nature of writing within the research process, and some of the problems and experiences of writing reported by research students. Finally, we will describe an intervention study examining the efficacy of different approaches to providing help with writing.

Writing difficulties experienced by research students

It is part of research student folklore that writing up is a time of stress, frustration and missed deadlines; but assessing the precise extent and nature of research students' writing problems is not easy. First, it is necessary to differentiate problems with writing *per se* from other sources of difficulty. The bulk of thesis writing tends to be concentrated in or beyond the final year of the research degree course which is often a time when motivation is flagging and other pressures are mounting. If a student is asked during this period about his or her writing experiences, the response is likely to be clouded by these other factors. Although many students who drop out of the PhD programmes do so during the writing-up period (Rudd 1985), this does not necessarily mean that writing difficulty itself was a decisive or even an important factor.

Second, many students may be reluctant to admit, or fail to recognise, that they have difficulties specifically with writing (Rudd 1985). Possibly, students who have failed to complete their theses are inclined to blame external rather than internal factors for the disappointing outcome of their research studies. Alternatively, writing may be perceived by students as unproblematic, because they conceptualise thesis writing in a narrow way as similar to the writing skills that they have already mastered prior to entering the research degree course. Confessing to difficulties with writing, therefore, may be perceived as an admission of fundamental incompetence. For this reason, students may well either play down the difficulties they experience or attribute them to factors other than lack of writing skill.

There is, however, good reason to suspect that writing a thesis can present difficulties, not least because it is so different in many ways from writing at an undergraduate level. Most undergraduate essays are relatively short, are written within a narrow time constraint and review a limited literature which is often detailed along with the essay topic. Most theses are many times longer than undergraduate essays, but the amount of time available for writing is also greater. False starts are thus less disastrous than when writing undergraduate essays, giving greater scope for experimentation. Most undergraduate essays review existing ideas, whereas the ideas contained within a thesis are expected to be, in some sense, original (but see Chapter 7). It is probably also the case that, to a much greater extent than for undergraduate essays, the rhetoric used to express these ideas is expected to conform to the norms of the academic community for whom the thesis is written.

It would seem reasonable to conclude, therefore, that completing a thesis requires skills different from those required for undergraduate writing. If this is the case, then it is probable that many students will experience difficulties in adjusting their writing to the demands of a research thesis.

In addition to lack of appropriate writing skills, students may experience problems when they actually commence writing and become excessively worried by what they perceive to be the demands of the task facing them. The sheer scale of the writing task, for example, may itself be a source of anxiety and thus procrastination. Similarly, some students may be hindered in their writing not so much by an inability to produce good quality text, but by excessive concern as to whether or not what they write is, in fact, in an acceptable style or sounds sufficiently 'academic' (Bartholomae 1985). Academic writing for research students may in many ways be similar to any other situation in which a novice has to speak in front of a group of experts, and thus brings with it the same self conscious-ness and fear of 'saying the wrong thing'. This anxiety may result in writer's block (Rose 1980). Worry about correct expression, as we discuss below, may also present problems for the student if it leads to a premature concern with expression at the expense of content.

There is indirect evidence that, for whatever reasons, some re-search students do experience writing difficulties. Rudd (1985) in interviews with failed or delayed PhD students found few who would directly admit to having difficulty expressing their ideas as text. Nevertheless, several of his interviewees described having dif-ficulties with converting the material they had collected during research into a thesis. Problems often centred around extracting central themes and logical progressions on which to build a coherent thesis. Interestingly, several of these students seemed to see a strict demarcation between collecting data, or doing research, and the writing up of this material as a thesis. It is possible that this perception may itself be a cause of problems (see below).

Our own research (Torrance, Thomas and Robinson 1992 and in press) has confirmed that a substantial minority of students report difficulties with writing. We surveyed 228 full-time, UK domiciled social science research students about their writing experiences and habits. Of the 110 that replied, 80 per cent stated that they gained some degree of pleasure from writing, although only 26 per cent said that they did not find writing hard work. In itself, finding writing hard work clearly does not constitute a problem; research suggests that very few find writing easy (e.g. Plimpton 1963, Hartley and Knapper 1984). There were, however, a minority of students in our sample who seemed to experience serious difficulties with writing. Thirty-four per cent stated that they found writing highly stressful, 27 per cent found writing frustrating, and 21 per cent thought that the difficulties they experienced with writing might jeopardise the successfully completion of their PhDs. In total, approximately 50 per cent of the students we surveyed seemed to experience some sort of writing related problem, although relatively few (14%) described themselves as poor writers (see also Weir 1988).

Another index of the extent to which students experience difficul-ties with writing is their willingness to seek help. As part of a project evaluating different approaches to writing instruction for research students (Torrance, Thomas and Robinson 1993) which we describe below, we advertised short writing courses at several different UK universities. We found that around 25 per cent of the students that we contacted expressed an interest in participating. Thus, whatever the extent to which social science research students are prepared to admit to experiencing writing problems, a substantial minority believed that they could gain from a short course of writing instruction.

The role of writing in the research process

In order to understand why writing can be a problem, and what kind of instruction might be effective, it may help to examine the nature of research writing, and the role it can play in the research process.

Traditionally, writing skill has often been construed as the ability to express preconceived ideas in a way that makes them understandable to the reader. This is premised on an account of the writing process in which content is decided upon as an activity prior to the act of writing. This two-stage account is exemplified by the following anonymous quotation (recorded by Elbow 1973):

> In order to form good style, the primary rule and condition is not to attempt to express ourselves in language before we thoroughly know our meaning.

The author of this quotation not only saw a strict demarcation between developing ideas and expressing them, but also saw the first stage – the development of ideas – as the most important. Clear thinking and good ideas are, of course, important elements of the thesis-writing process. Several theorists have argued, however, that it is both incorrect and unhelpful to see the having of ideas and the expressing of these as text as discrete and unrelated activities.

Research texts (journal articles, books, theses) typically are not accurate records of the actions and findings of the researcher (Medawar 1964). Research writing is not simply a description of the researcher's activities, but a constructive process that uses research findings as raw materials to build one of several possible accounts of a programme of research. In the course of writing the researcher makes decisions about what audience to aim his or her account at, what results to report, the theoretical framework in which to set the account, what conclusions to draw and so forth. Each of these decisions constrains not only the rhetoric but also the meaning of the text that is produced. Research writing is, therefore, not simply a communication of knowledge but a negotiation of knowledge claims (Myers 1988; see also Bazerman 1983, Bizzell 1982).

The writing-up stage of the research process, viewed in this way, offers doctoral students both frustration and hope. Research writing, as a constructive activity, is likely to require as much if not more cognitive effort than the design and implementation stages of research. Consequently, students such as those interviewed by Rudd

(1985) who see the main aim of their PhD as data collection will find writing up unexpectedly difficult.

More positively, because of its constructive nature, research writing offers the possibility of making up for deficiencies or failings in the earlier stages of the PhD. It is not unusual, for example, for research students to find when they come to write their thesis that the research that they have conducted does not conclusively test the theory or explore the issue that they had set out to examine. According to the traditional two-stage conception of writing, a student in this position is in quite serious difficulties; an error has occurred in the first, content collecting phase of the writing process and, thus, cannot be corrected without collecting more data. Experienced researchers, however, can often successfully write up flawed research by, for example, reconstructing new research aims which the originally inconclusive results can fulfil. This is particularly true within the social sciences where critical tests are rare. Incidentally, the fact that it is often only when writing up that theoretical complications or inadequacies in the research design come to light in itself bears witness to the facilitation of thought by writing.

We would argue, therefore, that the process of writing is integral to the research process as a whole. If this is true, then it has implications both for discussions about the extent to which research students experience writing-related problems, and for the ways in which these problems might be remedied.

Understanding the writing problems of postgraduate students

Given the important role that writing can play in the research process, it seems desirable to determine in more detail the nature of the writing problems experienced by research students so that appropriate assistance and training can be provided. In our survey of research students' writing experiences we asked questions about their writing strategies and techniques as well as the writing problems they had encountered (Torrance *et al.* 1992). Our aim was to try to discover whether some writing strategies are more effective than others for the academic writing undertaken by research students.

The term writing strategy in this context refers to the way in which a writer partitions the task of writing into more manageable components, and the sequence in which these components are executed. Traditional approaches to writing typically involve a think-then-write strategy in which content is decided largely in advance of composing text. This is the strategy that is most often taught in British schools and recommended in student guides to studying (Torrance,

Thomas and Robinson 1991). It is not, however, typical of the way in which many experienced writers go about their writing. The think-then-write approach is, if anything, more typical of inexperienced writers.

Inexperienced writers typically decide content at an early stage in the writing process, either prior to or during the writing of a first draft (Faigley and Witte 1981, Perl 1979, Sommers 1980). Once the first draft has been written the content of the text is essentially fixed; any revisions the writer may make are purely cosmetic. Bereiter and Scardamalia (1987) have described this approach to writing as 'knowledge telling', because it involves little more than the transla-tion of preconceived meaning into an external representation in the form of text.

More experienced writers, by contrast, have usually become aware of the power of writing to develop their thinking (Faigley and Witte 1981, Sommers 1980). They thus adopt what Bereiter and Scardamalia (1987) have termed 'knowledge transforming' ap-proaches to writing. Briefly, Bereiter and Scardamalia suggest that the process of setting out ideas into sentences of full text can stimulate and develop thinking. The strategies employed in knowledge trans-forming may vary from writer to writer, but many postpone final decisions over content and structure of text till late in the writing process. Some writers produce a succession of rough drafts, others revise extensively. For most, writing is a recursive process in which planning, drafting and revising are interleaved (de Beaugrande 1984, Flower and Hayes 1981, Matsuhashi 1987, Nold 1981).

Experienced and inexperienced writers differ crucially in their attitudes to revision (Sommers 1980). For the inexperienced, revision is simply a matter of correcting mistakes. It is perceived as an activity that should be unnecessary if sufficient care is taken over the first draft. In contrast, experienced authors do not necessarily see revision in this negative way. Indeed they can see revision as a productive and even satisfying stage in the writing process during which they may discover new ideas and perspectives on their subject matter.

The complexity of the subject matter and the sheer length of a thesis means that it may be impracticable to use a planning approach which determines content in advance. Furthermore, the constructive nature of much research writing seems more likely to require a knowledge-transforming than a knowledge-telling writing strategy. It would seem that most school-level advice on writing appears to emphasise the latter, and that many undergraduate writing tasks can also be completed successfully by knowledge telling. Given all this, we might then expect that one particular obstacle facing many re search students is to discard knowledge-telling conceptions and strategies and develop a knowledge-transforming approach instead.

In the aggregate, the research students in our survey were in fact intermediate between novices and experienced writers in the strategies they adopted (Torrance *et al.* 1992). Like experienced writers, the research students had generally realised that several drafts were normally necessary to produce an acceptable academic document. The research students, however, were more like novices in their comments about revision. Most described revision as a way of improving expression and correcting mistakes; only a few commented that changing content was an aim of their revision. One possible interpretation of this pattern of results is that the research students were in the process of discovering a 'knowledge-transforming' approach to writing, but some still retained 'knowledge-telling' habits and attitudes.

The next step in the analysis of our survey results was to examine more closely the relation between writing strategy and writing experiences and productivity (see Torrance *et al.* in press). To do this we performed a cluster analysis on the research students' responses to our questions about writing strategies. These questions focused particularly on the activities that students engaged in when writing, how clear they needed their thinking to be before starting to write, and their reasons for revising. The best solution to an agglomerative, hierarchical cluster analysis of the students' responses to the strategy questions identified three similarly-sized and distinct groups of students. The statistically significant differences in strategy among the clusters centred around two factors: first, the stage in the writing process at which students took decisions about the content and structure of their text, and second, the number of drafts written in preparing a piece of text.

The members of the first cluster generally preferred to have their ideas clear before starting to write, and tended to write fewer drafts than members of the other two clusters. Only a very few reported that changing content was a reason for revising their text. These students seem best described as planners, because their approach to writing appears to match closely the traditional think-then-write strategy described above.

The members of the second cluster generally preferred to start writing before taking final decisions about content. These students were significantly more likely than the other groups to report that writing clarified their understanding of their own arguments. They also tended to write more drafts than the planners and were more likely to report that their main aim when revising was to change content. They seemed therefore to have discovered the 'knowledge transforming' possibilities of writing. We will refer to them as 'revisers'.

The strategies typical of the third cluster did not present such a coherent picture. Like the planners, members of this group preferred to plan content in advance of writing. Unlike the planners, however, students in this cluster reported producing more drafts than even the revisers, and were more likely to report that they changed content when they revised. It seems that students in this group started by trying to plan their text, and then found themselves forced into content changes during revision. We termed these 'mixed strategy writers'.

We then tried to ascertain whether there were any differences among the strategy clusters in terms of writing productivity and reported difficulty with writing. Practical limitations on our resources forced us to rely on self reports of both productivity and problems. These subjective estimates can only be approximate, but they may still provide a useful basis for comparing the three strategy clusters because it is unlikely that estimation errors will have differed systematically across the clusters. (Furthermore, the interventions necessary to collect objective data on writing productivity could have so disrupted the research students' normal working environment as to seriously undermine the validity on any data so collected.)

Our self-report data suggested that the planners were significantly more productive than were the other two groups (measured in terms of the ratio of the words reported written to the number of hours spent writing during the three months prior to receiving the questionnaire). There were no differences between the planners and revisers in terms of their enjoyment of writing, their satisfaction with the finished product or in their experience of writing difficulties.

These results do not, of course, conclusively demonstrate a causal link between students' writing strategies and the problems they reported in our survey. We think it plausible, however, that both planners and revisers had adopted successful writing strategies, with the planners enjoying higher productivity. This result confirms that some individuals can successfully employ what appears to be a knowledge-telling approach (see also Hartley and Branthwaite 1989, Kellogg 1986), but that a knowledge-transforming approach involving extensive revision can also be successful (if more time consuming).

The mixed strategy writers, however, seemed to have been less fortunate in their writing experiences. These students were more likely than members of both the other two groups to state that worry about writing prevented them from producing text, and were also more likely to see writing difficulties as jeopardising the completion of their degrees. They also rated writing as significantly more difficult than did the planners (but not the revisers). In short, the planners and revisers seem to be using different but effective writing strategies. In contrast, the mixed strategy writers present a picture of students without a coherent strategy for writing and experiencing difficulties and anxiety about their writing performance.

To conclude, much research indicates that inexperienced and experienced writers differ quite markedly in their conceptions of writing (knowledge telling versus knowledge transforming) and also in their strategies for writing expository academic text. There is some evidence from our own research that a planning strategy may be more efficient (see also Hartley and Branthwaite 1989, Kellogg 1986), but it is probably a mistake to conclude that a planning strategy is best for everyone. One powerful argument against such a conclusion is that most writers are originally taught a planning strategy as school children. It seems unlikely that the many accomplished writers who evolve alternative strategies to planning would do so if they had found that planning had consistently worked for them. The mixed-strategy writers in our survey were also writers for whom planning was apparently unsuccessful. We are unable as yet to offer a complete explanation as to why planning text works for some students but not for others. As indicated above, the nature of the writing task faced by individual students may differ and partly determine the best approach to writing. It seems to us likely, for example, that writing up routine research which lies within a well-established theoretical framework may be more amenable to a knowledge-telling approach than writing a thesis which develops new theoretical ideas or explores competing conceptualisations. In addition, it is conceivable that individual differences in cognitive style may also predispose some individuals towards one writing strategy rather than another (Wason 1985). Further work is needed to explore these issues.

Nevertheless, our results allow two tentative conclusions for writing instruction. First, it seems wise to allow for individual variations in writing strategies, and second, it may be important to alert students who are unsuccessful when using a think-then-write approach to knowledge-transforming alternatives.

An evaluation of three conceptual approaches to writing instruction

Apart from the material already discussed above, we could find very little published work to guide us in our attempts to evaluate the potential benefits of writing instruction for research students. Postgraduate research training in British universities has until recently included little formal instruction on academic writing (Torrance *et al.* 1992), and we could find no published work evaluating instruction on writing specifically for research students. There is a substantial North American literature on the effects of writing instruction for undergraduates (see Hillocks 1984), but its relevance to research students is debatable.

As we have already noted, traditional approaches to writing suggest that the main requirements for success are first to generate appropriate content, and second, to express it in an acceptable form. Problems at the first stage could be addressed by instruction on planning, problems at the second by teaching correct English usage, good style and clarity. A more radical approach to instruction could address students' conceptions of their writing, and introduce them to knowledge-transforming alternatives to the traditional think-then-write strategy (see above). Our survey research suggested that this third possibility might be appropriate to the needs of a significant number of research students, but we could not rule out the possibility that more traditional instruction might also be helpful. Consequently, we went back to first principles and devised three conceptually distinct approaches to writing instruction based on the considerations outlined above. These approaches were then embodied in three writing courses which we called the product-centred course, the cognitive strategies course and the generative writing and shared revision course.

The product-centred course

This course, as its name suggests, focused on the structural features of academic texts. The content of the course was a combination of 'rules for good English' of the sort presented in traditional style manuals (e.g., Gowers 1986, Gunning 1968, Strunk and White 1979), rules for correct academic writing (e.g., Turabian 1987), and the findings of applied linguistic research into the structure of academic text (Dudley-Evans and Hopkins 1988, Swales 1984). The rules and examples of good style and correct usage probably need no further introduction here. Swales' analyses of academic texts may be less familiar, although they have been used particularly in the teaching of English to overseas students. In brief, Swales has identified a number of 'moves', that are typically made in certain kinds of academic text. Introductions to scientific articles reporting research findings, for example, can be considered a distinct literary genre. Generally, acceptable article introductions contain a number of implicit or explicit 'moves' in the development of the scientific case for conducting the research to be reported. In our product-centred writing course we taught the students quite explicitly about the key 'moves' for a variety of genres of scientific writing.

The course was divided into a number of short sections, each consisting of a brief talk to introduce the principle or rule to be learned followed by exercises to illustrate and give practice in its application. By considering only the required structure of the final written product, this course was entirely neutral with regard to writing strategies, and in presenting the course we took no stand on knowledge-telling versus knowledge-transforming approaches.

The cognitive strategies course

In contrast to the product-centred course, this course aimed to offer the students strategies for developing their thinking prior to, or independently of, producing full text. As such the course promoted the think-then-write approach to writing. Our intention was that, during the course, students would develop a 'tool kit' of cognitive strategies that could be applied at appropriate times during the construction of a document. This course drew heavily on work by Flower and Hayes (1977) and by Flower (1989). We introduced a variety of different strategies or heuristics for generating and structuring content (e.g., brainstorming, concept mapping, construction issue trees; see Flower 1989, Gowin 1981). The course also presented strategies for adapting text to conform to the needs and expectations of a specific readership (e.g., arguing with an imagined audience, audience analysis).

After receiving instruction on each strategy the students were given an opportunity to practise its use in developing a piece of writing of their own choice. This was drawn, in most cases, from their own thesis work. In short, this course fostered a plan-centred approach: it aimed to provide students with cognitive strategies for clarifying their ideas prior to composing text.

The generative writing and shared revision course

In this course we attempted to combine a knowledge-transforming approach to writing with an understanding of writing as a negotiation of knowledge claims with imagined or real readers. The course was divided into two parts of roughly equal length. First, students produced a 'pre-draft' of a piece of text related to their thesis work using a generative writing strategy (Wason 1985). They were instructed to write in full prose, without pausing for thought or worrying too much about producing text that was stylistically correct or error free. They then revised this rough text to produce a working draft which, although by no means polished, was at least intelligible to other readers. The strategies for this part of the course were similar to those suggested by Elbow (1981).

The second part of the course was taken up with reviewing and revising this working draft. It comprised several exercises in which the student received comments on their texts from other students. The exercises included discussion of a version of one of the working drafts that had been re-written by an experienced academic writer (a technique described by Cohen 1983) and a 'comment while you read' exercise in which a partner read a student's text out loud to him or her, making comments as they read (adapted from Johnston 1987). Students also made detailed written comments on each other's texts. We encouraged the students to think of other people's comments on their texts not as corrections but as raw material which, combined with the working draft, could be built into another, more developed version of the piece that they were writing.

Evaluation

In order to gain some indication of the relative efficacy of these three approaches to postgraduate writing instruction we conducted each course twice, in late 1990 and early 1991, with different students attending each time. Each course was run over two consecutive days and involved approximately seven hours of teaching time (including exercises).

Students attended the courses voluntarily and not as a requirement of their research degree programmes. So as to ensure an approximately random distribution of students across the courses, all three were advertised in the same way and without giving details of course content. A total of 104 students participated in the study with 41 students completing the product-centred course, 30 completing the cognitive strategies course and 33 completing the generative writing course. Fifty-two students were studying part-time, and the remaining full-time students were roughly equally distributed between first, second and third year of study. Twenty-two of the students did not speak English as a first language. The data obtained from these students were, however, not significantly different from those of the remainder. The students were drawn from a wide range of social science disciplines with a slight bias towards education (33 students).

The students' own impressions of the effectiveness of their course were assessed by means of two questionnaires, one administered immediately after the course, and one ten to twelve weeks later. These asked both how helpful the course had been with specific aspects of the writing process, and for a global rating of the course's usefulness.

A detailed analysis of the results is reported in Torrance *et al.* (1993). In general, all three courses were perceived as useful, the product-centred course being rated as slightly less useful than the other two courses in providing help with developing thinking and with expressing ideas.

Perhaps more important than the students' immediate reactions is their considered evaluation of the course once they have had an opportunity to put into practice what was taught. Seventy-two students completed the follow-up questionnaire, of whom fourteen reported not having done any writing since the course. The latter were dropped from further analysis. The remaining students' responses to this questionnaire suggested that, in practice, the courses were less useful than they had at first anticipated, although the differences between the two ratings were in no case very large. The one exception to this pattern was the response of students who had attended the generative writing course to the question 'how helpful did you find the course was in getting started on a piece of writing?' Their replies showed a small but significant increase on their previous rating suggesting that, when put into practice, the generative approach to writing was found to be of more use than they had at first anticipated.

Improvements in the quality of the text that students produced as a result of attending the course were assessed by asking them to produce a short, polished piece of writing at the start and at the end of the course. These were on topics of the students' own choosing, related to their thesis work. Global ratings of the quality of the text that the students produced showed no significant change during any of the courses. This result was, perhaps, to be expected. Obtaining reliable measures of text quality is notoriously difficult (see, for example, Charney 1984). This, combined with the timing of the post test – immediately after two days of quite intensive instruction – and the artificiality of the writing task, made it unlikely that we would detect what are likely to have been at most quite subtle improvements in the students' ability to produce good quality text. We did, however, estimate the readability of the writing samples by calculating Flesch counts (Flesch 1948) and found improvements in readability for essays written after the product-centred and the generative writing courses, but not in the essays written after the cognitive strategies course. Quite how good an index of readability the Flesch count is, or how readability assessed in this way is related to writing quality in general, is a matter of debate (e.g., Croll and Moskaluk 1977). However, this result is of some interest in itself given that rules for readability were only taught as part of the product-centred course.

Writing productivity is perhaps more important a measure of a course's usefulness than either the students' evaluation of the course or its effects on the quality of the students' writing. Supervisors' comments on drafts are an effective way of ensuring that a certain quality of writing is eventually achieved and, consequently, adequately supervised PhDs are rarely if ever failed because the thesis is badly written. Supervisors, however, have a much harder job in ensuring that their students are sufficiently productive to complete on time. Arguably, therefore, writing instruction for research students will be of most service if it increases students' productivity.

We measured productivity as in the previous study by asking students immediately prior to the course and ten to twelve weeks after completing the course to estimate how much thesis-related text they had produced in the preceding three months. The factors affecting the accuracy of these estimates were presumably equal across all three courses (see above). The effects of the courses on students' productivity are described in detail by Torrance *et al.* (1993). In general, however, students who attended the product-centred and generative writing courses showed significant increases in their productivity but this was not the case for students who attended the cognitive strategies course.

The evaluation data taken together indicate that both the product-centred and generative writing course had positive benefits, but that the cognitive strategies course was unhelpful, despite its positive rating from the students who received it. While conclusions must remain tentative these results seem to be consistent with claims that we made earlier in this chapter. We argued that writing is a constructive process in which ideas are selected and developed for presentation to a particular audience. If this is so, then instruction is more likely to be effective if it promotes a knowledge-transforming approach to writing; hence the success of the generative writing course. Similarly, the apparent failure of the cognitive strategies course to have any effect on the students' productivity may stem at least in part from its knowledge-telling orientation. This conclusion is reinforced by consideration of the mixed-strategy writers in our survey (see above). These students were experiencing problems using a planning approach to their writing. If the problems of students in this position stemmed from inadequate planning rather than because a planning approach was inappropriate for them, then we would have expected instruction on the sophisticated planning strategies presented in the cognitive strategies course to have increased writing productivity. That it failed to do so is consistent with the conclusion that it is the plan-centred approach itself rather than the inadequate execution of planning strategies that is the problem for these students.

We have also suggested above that excessive concern about producing text that is stylistically acceptable to the academic community can be debilitating. If these claims are true then writing instruction will be most effective either if it focuses students' attention away from stylistic demands of the audience during the initial stage of writing while ideas are being developed or if it tackles the students' concerns directly by teaching them the stylistic rules they need to talk with confidence to their audience. These solutions were, arguably, provided by the generative writing and product-centred courses respectively.

The generative writing technique, by focusing attention away from rhetorical demands in the first stage of writing, gives relatively unhindered scope for idea selection and organisation (Elbow 1987). In the second stage of the workshop, when stylistic constraints were introduced, the students already had fairly well developed sets of ideas. The difference between this approach and that suggested in the cognitive strategies course is that these ideas were expressed in text which could be fairly readily modified to improve the style. Writers who employ the think-then-write approach advocated in the cognitive strategies course will, at this stage, still be faced with the problem of putting pen to paper, which for students is where fears about getting the style right are likely to surface.

The product-centred course tackled the 'fear of speaking out' problem from the other end. By teaching rules for academic style, this approach should increase students' confidence sufficiently for concern about being stylistically correct not to inhibit their writing. The apparent success of the product-centred course is, in itself, interesting given that this form of instruction is ineffective for students at or below the first year undergraduate level (Hillocks 1984, White 1989).

Conclusions for research training

Until recently, few institutions have provided formal instruction on writing (or any other kind of formal training) for their research students. Only 20 per cent of the second and third year students who responded to our survey (conducted in late 1989 and early 1990) reported having received writing instruction through a class or workshop and only 42 per cent reported having received help with writing from any source, including their supervisor. What instruction they had received seemed to have focused more on strategies for writing (how to plan, revise and so forth) than on what the finished thesis should look like.

Attitudes towards training for research students however may, of necessity, be changing. With increased emphasis both on completion rates and on the marketability of the skills acquired as a result of completing a PhD there has been an associated move towards including a formally taught component in research degree programmes. It may well be that since we conducted our survey more departments have incorporated some form of formal writing instruction into their research degree courses.

Our results suggest that even quite short courses of writing instruction offer benefits for postgraduate research students in the social sciences. They suggest also that some writing problems may be sufficiently similar in different disciplines so that general writing courses can be helpful. This is not to say that courses are best conducted at this level. Since stylistic norms vary considerably from discipline to discipline, instruction for students studying within the same discipline could be tailored more closely to their particular needs and this should result in greater improvement in their writing skill. However, not all departments have sufficient numbers of research students to make this a feasible option. Our results suggest that even if instruction must, of necessity, be aimed at students from a range of social science subjects, it can still be effective.

Exactly what form this writing instruction should take will depend in part on the resources and expertise available to the departments or faculties for whose students the instruction is conducted. Our research suggests that instruction should not be too prescriptive but should allow for variations in approach. In the absence of adequate diagnoses of students' needs on an individual basis, the best approach may well be to incorporate a variety of forms of instruction within a single course and let the students themselves decide what best meets their current requirements. Our results suggest, however, that whatever form the instruction takes, it should focus on the production of text, and not solely on the sorting out of ideas prior to putting pen to paper. Until further research clarifies the picture there would seem to be distinct benefits from both instructing students on rhetoric and in enlarging their conceptions of the writing process to include knowledge-transforming approaches.

Acknowledgment

We gratefully acknowledge the support of both the Economic and Social Research Council, UK (award number T007 40 1005), and the Nuffield Foundation. Any views expressed, however, are those of the authors and do not necessarily reflect the views of these organisations.

References

Bartholomae, D. (1985) Inventing the university. In M. Rose (ed) *When a Writer Can't Write: Studies in Writer's Block and Other Composition Disorders.* New York: Guildford.

Bazerman, C. (1983) Scientific writing as a social act: A review of the literature in the sociology of science. In C.R. Miller, P.V. Anderson and R.J. Brockman (eds) *New Essays in Scientific and Technical Communication.* Farmingdale, N.Y.: Baywood Publishing Co. pp.157–184.

Bereiter, C. and Scardamalia, M. (1987) *The Psychology of Written Composition.* Hillsdale, New Jersey: Erlbaum.

Bizzell, P. (1982) Cognition, convention and certainty: what we need to know about writing. *Pre/text 3,* 213–244.

Charney, D. (1984) The validity of using holistic scoring to evaluate writing: a critical overview. *Research in the Teaching of English 18,* 65–81.

Cohen, A.D. (1983) Reformulating compositions. *TESOL Newsletter XVII, 6,* 1–5.

Croll, W. and Moskaluk, S. (1977) Should flesch counts count? *Teaching of Psychology 4,* 48–49.

De Beaugrande, R. (1984) *Text Production.* Norwood: Ablex.

Elbow, P. (1973) *Writing Without Teachers.* Oxford: Oxford University Press.

Elbow, P. (1981) *Writing With Power: Techniques for Mastering the Writing Process.* Oxford: Oxford University Press.

Elbow, P. (1987) Closing my eyes as I speak: an argument for ignoring audience. *College English 49,* 50–69.

Faigley, L. and Witte, S.P. (1981) Analyzing revision. *College Composition and Communication 32,* 400–414.

Flesch, R. (1948) A new readability yardstick. *Journal of Applied Psychology 32,* 221–233.

Flower, L. (1989) *Problem Solving Strategies for Writing.* (3rd edition). Orlando, Fl.: Harcourt Brace Jovanovich.

Flower, L. and Hayes, J. (1977) Problem solving strategies and the writing process. *College English 39,* 449–461.

Flower, L. and Hayes, J. (1981) A cognitive process theory of writing. *College Composition and Communication 32,* 365–387.

Gowers, E. (1986) *The Complete Plain Words* (3rd edition, revised by S. Greenbaum and J. Whitcut). London: HMSO.

Gowin, D.B. (1981) *Educating.* Ithaca, N.Y.: Cornell University Press.

Gunning, R. (1968) *The Technique of Clear Writing.* (revised edition), New York: McGraw-Hill.

Hartley, J. and Branthwaite, A. (1989) The psychologist as wordsmith: A questionnaire study of the writing strategies of productive British psychologists. *Higher Education 18*, 423–452.

Hartley, J. and Knapper, C.K. (1984) Academics and their writing. *Studies in Higher Education 9*, 151–167.

Hillocks, G. (1984) What works in teaching composition: a meta-analysis of experimental treatment studies. *American Journal of Education*, November, 133–170.

Hopkins, A. and Dudley-Evans, T. (1988) A genre-based investigation of the discussion sections in articles and dissertations. *English for Specific Purposes 7*, 113–121.

Johnston, B. (1987) *Assessing English: Helping Students to Reflect on Their Own Work* (2nd edition), Milton Keynes: Open University Press.

Kellogg, R.T. (1986) Writing method and productivity of science and engineering faculty. *Research in Higher Education 25*, 147–163.

Matsuhashi, A. (1987) Revising the plan and altering the text. In A. Matsuhashi (ed) *Writing in Real Time.* Norwood: Ablex.

Medawar, P.B. (1964) Is the scientific paper fraudulent? *Saturday Review*, August 1st, 42–43.

Myers, G. (1988) The social construction of science and the teaching of English. In P. Robinson (ed) *Academic Writing: Process and Product.* London: Modern English Publications.

Nold, E.W. (1981) Revising. In C.H. Frederiksen and J.F. Dominic (eds) *Writing: The Nature, Development and Teaching of Written Communication, Volume 2. Writing: Process, Development and Communication.* Hillsdale, N.J.: Erlbaum.

Perl, S. (1979) The composing process of unskilled college writers. *Research in the Teaching of English 13*, 314–336.

Plimpton, G. (1963) (ed) *Writers at Work: The Paris Review Interviews, Second Series.* New York: Viking.

Rose, M. (1980) Rigid rules, inflexible plans and the stifling of language: A cognitivist analysis of writers block. *College Composition and Communication 31*, 389–401.

Rudd, E. (1985) *A New Look at Postgraduate Failure.* Guildford: Society for Research into Higher Education.

Sommers, N. (1980) Revision strategies of student writers and experienced adult writers. *College Composition and Communication 31*, 378–388.

Strunk, W. Jr. and White, E.B. (1979) *The Elements of Style (3rd edition).* New York: Macmillan.

Swales, J. (1984) Research into the structure of introductions to journal articles and its application to the teaching of academic writing. In R. Williams, J. Swales and J. Kirkman (eds) *Common Ground: Shared interests in ESP and Communication Studies*. Oxford: Pergamon.

Torrance, M., Thomas, G.V. and Robinson, E.J. (1991) Strategies for answering examination essay questions: Is it helpful to write a plan?. *British Journal of Educational Psychology 61*, 46–54.

Torrance, M., Thomas, G.V. and Robinson, E.J. (1992) The writing experiences of social science research students. *Studies in Higher Education 17*, 155–167.

Torrance, M., Thomas, G.V. and Robinson, E.J. (1993) Training in research writing: An evaluation of three conceptual orientations. *British Journal of Educational Psychology 63*, 170–184.

Torrance, M., Thomas, G.V. and Robinson, E.J. (in press) The writing strategies of graduate research students in the social sciences. *Higher Education*.

Turabian, K. (1987) *A Manual for Writers of Term Papers, Theses and Dissertations* (5th edition). Chicago: Chicago University Press.

Wason, P.C. (1985) How to write an essay. *The New Psychologist*, May, 16–19.

Wason, P.C. (1970) On writing scientific papers. *Physics Bulletin 21*, 407–408.

Weir, C. (1988) Academic writing: Can we please all the people all the time?. In P. Robinson (ed) *Academic Writing: Process and Product*. London: Modern English Publications.

White, E. (1989) *Developing Successful College Writing Programmes*. California: Josey Bass.

Chapter 7

Quality in the PhD
Points at Which Quality May Be Assessed

Estelle M. Phillips

Introduction

This chapter examines the interpretation and practice of quality by both students and academic staff, including the most general standards of excellence looked for by examiners. Consideration is given to what students generally understand to be required of them and how this compares with the academic's expectations. These issues have a bearing on the overall idea of what constitutes quality in the PhD as well as the more detailed notion of how work is assessed as it progresses.

At the time that the research on which this chapter is based was started, very little had been done in the area of quality (as opposed to assessment) in education generally and the PhD in particular. In the intervening period, such ideas as 'quality control' and 'total quality management' have infiltrated from the industrial sector and there is now some literature in this area. See, for example, the CVCP Green Paper and the Government White Paper on Education (both 1991) where the notions of quality audit and quality assessment in higher education (including research education) are also discussed.

Nevertheless, quality remains a difficult concept to define. Despite this, academics do habitually make judgements of quality and other academics debate whether these are, in fact, quality judgements. It is therefore important to separate the concepts that have to do with the measurement and assessment of quality from the concept of quality itself.

The Oxford dictionary gives several different meanings for quality but the most relevant to the topic being discussed here are 'excellence' and 'to a standard' which are, nevertheless, a little tautological. Pirsig (1976) is rather more helpful. In his discussion of writing and composition, while he does not give an overall definition of quality, he does list some of the components. He says that decisions are made on the basis of relatively similar backgrounds and similar knowledge and speaks of 'unity or hanging togetherness; vividness; authority; economy; sensitivity; clarity; emphasis; flow; suspense; brilliance; precision; proportion; and depth' (p.202).

There is a suggestion of an aesthetic element contained in his approach which would accord with what is looked for in the overall assessment of a thesis because, when discussing quality, it is surely the case that the whole must be more than merely the sum of its component parts.

In fact, my own understanding of this concept within the framework of the PhD has to do with the notion of coherence. I have previously argued (Phillips 1991) the importance of writing with regard to the organisation of practical work and conceptualisation of the argument that links the different parts of the work together. In this connection, students and supervisors were asked about writing (and re-writing) drafts of the thesis. The answers to these questions will be discussed in some detail below.

The research attempted to understand better:

- the nature of the PhD;
- the experience of staff in assessing; and
- the experience of students in meeting standards of quality which are implicit, but are rarely made explicit, in the process of submitting and evaluating a PhD thesis.

There are, potentially, five opportunities for assessing quality during any period of registration for a research degree. These are at the point of:

1. Selecting the applicant into the system.
2. Upgrading the student from MPhil to PhD registration.
3. Continuous monitoring of work in progress.
4. Pre-examination or preparation for the viva.
5. The final examination/viva.

However, it became clear, as the work progressed, that not all institutions take advantage of these opportunities. This outcome led to suggestions for assessing the quality of individual research student projects as they developed (Phillips 1992).

The suggestions arose from the assumption that there *are* these specific points at which work can be influenced and the quality improved. As can be seen from Figure 7.1, these points may be perceived as the core within a context which is either enabling or debilitating. The context is, of course, the institution itself and the resources it provides for each department to offer its research students. The whole, i.e. core within context, is that from which a high (or low) quality PhD can emerge.

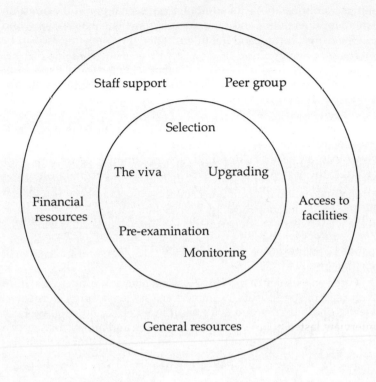

Figure 7.1: Quality in the PhD

The resources include:
- A. Staff support in the form of the academic supervisor(s), departmental research tutor or equivalent, and other academics in the student's own or other departments.
- B. Peer group in terms of the community of researchers in which the postgraduate is working.
- C. Access to facilities such as a desk; common room; technician.
- D. Provision of more general facilities, for example: the library; computing terminals.
- E. Financial resources to cover costs of, for example postage for questionnaires; travel and attendance at relevant conferences.

Within this context it is possible to influence the work that is carried out. The influence is most effective when it occurs at the specific points identified above. In addition the research posed the question whether supervisors and students discuss their expectations and whether they know what the other thinks they are supposed to be doing.

Overall, this study examined academics, departments and institutions to see whether anything was done by them to encourage the development of high quality in PhD research and its reporting.

The study

Four institutions, including one polytechnic, were studied. The selected institutions represented both high status universities with strong international reputations and those that had been blacklisted by the ESRC for not meeting submission standards. Within them there were twenty-six departments teaching eight social science disciplines, including anthropology, business studies, economics, geography, industrial relations, psychology, sociology and international relations.

Forty-one students and fifty-eight members of academic staff in their roles of supervisors, examiners and research tutors were interviewed individually and with assurances of confidentiality. Each interview lasted about one and a half hours and aimed to ascertain the criteria which examiners apply, and the expectations which students have, of the standard of excellence required in the PhD. Special attention was paid to the role of external examiner.

The interviews were semi-structured and open ended. In addition to the interviews, there were two group discussions covering the same topics. One group comprised 8 members of staff; the other 12 postgraduate research students. Members of academic staff and social science students at different points in their registration were selected to ensure diversity rather than for statistical representativeness.

The table below shows the distribution of students participating in the study and where they were in the registration period for a research degree:

Year of Registration	Number of Students
First	9
Second	8
Third	12
Fourth	10
Completed	2

The gender distribution of the sample of people interviewed is given below:

Gender	Staff	Student
Male	49	23
Female	9	18

Research results

Selection into the system

The selection point is vital to the ultimate quality of the finished PhD because it is at the point of entry that the limits of what, ultimately, will be possible are set. Accepting students who have the potential to complete their research and write their theses to the required standard within given deadlines is a prerequisite for institutions who wish to satisfy research council demands while maintaining the quality of the finished product.

The four institutions differed in the extent to which they had formalised their approach to research degrees and the people involved in them. Two institutions and several departments had 'Guidelines' setting out detailed instructions which covered different procedures to be employed with regard to the various stages of a research degree (including selection, upgrading/transfer, supervisory practices and, in some cases, formal contracts between supervisor and student). The printed regulations from the higher degrees committees of those departments/institutions who had formulated policy statements, together with the content analysis of interviews, showed that there is considerable variation with regard to selection practices.

Some institutions have quite elaborate procedures including a requirement for an acceptable research proposal from the student; some insist on successful completion of the departmental taught postgraduate course; some departments require personal interviews with one or more members of staff – although it is important to note that not all students who are accepted for a research degree are interviewed. Other institutions merely insist on specific grades (1st or 2/1) in the undergraduate degree or a good Master's degree. This, even though we have known for more than 30 years that there is no correlation between success in research and a good pass in the examination system (Hudson 1960, 1977, Miller 1970).

In the UK at present selection is closely related to funding and students from overseas bring in more revenue than British students. There is also consideration given to University Funding Committee quotas which sometimes result in acceptable British students being refused, due to lack of financial support as the following quotations from some of the supervisor interviews demonstrate:

> We're in business for overseas students. UK students can't even pay high fees if they wanted to. We can take any number of high fee students but we're limited on low fee places. (Philosophy)

> We mustn't just take students for cash generation, it's a moral issue. (Business School)

> We can't accept all we'd like to accept. We reached the low fee quota very early this year and had to put good people on the waiting list. The high fee people go through the same process but don't have the barriers to acceptance of the home, low fee, students. (Sociology)

These barriers to the selection of some acceptable students are in addition to those where no suitable member of staff is available to supervise a promising applicant with a good proposal.

In addition, the importance of language training for students from overseas is often not emphasised at the point of selection into the system. Overseas students should be encouraged from the start of their course to do something about improving their command of English grammar. It is important for them to be aware of precisely what is needed for an acceptable thesis to be written to the required standard. Too often, it appears that any focus on the standard of written English required is left until the research work is almost completed.

Upgrading from MPhil to PhD registration as an opportunity to contribute to the 'Assessment of quality'

The research results showed that there is wide variety in how this part of the process is handled. This variety was apparent at departmental level as well as between different institutions. It was at the point of upgrading that differences in organisational approaches were most obvious. More specifically in eleven departments, plus the whole of the polytechnic, transfer from MPhil to PhD was extremely rigorous.

In these cases formal upgrading procedures were in force at either an institutional or departmental level. Such procedures included mandatory written papers and, in some cases, a panel interview based on the written work. In the polytechnic, CNAA regulations had to be adhered to and accounted for a very high degree of formality as well as the length of time it took for transfer to be achieved.

Here respondents explained that in order to be upgraded according to the regulations it was necessary to produce:

a hefty document and the decision is made on the basis of the document. Then there is a meeting at which questions are asked and minutes taken. A letter is sent a few weeks later.

When describing the make-up of the panel it became clear that it was not necessarily peopled by subject specialists:

There is at least one expert on the topic, but it is a rigorous examination by people who know nothing of the field.

It was described by some supervisors as 'an excellent system' and 'a useful quality control hurdle'. Others referred to it in less agreeable ways:

Some people take their moment, or rather hours, of glory by deeply nitpicking what's happening in other departments.

Students were not too happy with the assumptions underlying the panel's questions:

Then there's the problem of saying what *extra* you're going to do. It assumes a quantitative approach and you need to play to bureaucracy with regard to the important *visible extra* amount.

Nor did things always go as they originally intended:

One student had an appalling experience, not all the panel had read the paper but they still asked questions. The candidate had to rewrite incorporating their comments. It's bureaucratic power rather than learning points.

One supervisor summed it up as being 'a good system in theory but not always in practice, it depends on getting the right people.'

In contrast to the above, there were three departments who merely upgraded students after a year or 18 months in order to satisfy funding requirements and four supervisors who upgraded their students when they thought they merited it, but without necessarily informing the student that they had done so. One supervisor saw it as irrelevant and waited until students were ready to submit before arranging a retrospective upgrading.

These different approaches mean that not all students are given sufficient information regarding what is required of them and some departments/supervisors miss the opportunity to influence outcomes. The procedure adopted in upgrading students from MPhil to PhD status is important as it is (or could be) the first step in the examination process and will, therefore, give some clue to the standard set by the department or institution. It can also provide important information to the institution regarding the potential quality of the final outcome and identify the development of any problems that may need to be confronted in the future.

Monitoring work in progress

Knowing how students and their work are progressing at regular intervals during the course of the registration period can be a useful way of identifying difficulties at an early stage and allows for help and encouragement to be given when required. One member of staff explained the importance of monitoring in this way:

> the hardest thing for the PhD student is to know if what they are doing is what is required.

Annual report forms are becoming more widely used, but are not yet required practice in all departments. Even where they are, the methods used to complete them vary. The questions asked in this part of the research included: Do students write a preliminary report of their own work? Should supervisors base their comments on what the student has said? Do students (if they are involved) write about their progress in the past and plans for the future on the same form as their supervisor?

Results of the qualitative analysis showed that practices varied even within departments. Some supervisors merely wrote a perfunctory note on their student's progress; some required a formal report from the students of their own work on which the supervisor could base his or her report. Where they were used, the report forms were usually processed through the department for onward transmission to the Dean of Research or equivalent.

Pre-examination and preparation for viva as an opportunity to raise quality standards

Moving now from potential methods of controlling, influencing and assessing quality, the research also attempted to obtain some insight into what is perceived to constitute aspects of quality in the PhD itself. This part of the study was concerned with the process of thesis submission (or pre-examination). Knowledge of what happens at this point, if anything, is important for future policy decisions regarding how much guidance could be given to students in the final stages of registration.

The questions in this section were aimed at discovering at what stage supervisors see drafts of the thesis and whether their decisions with regard to asking for revisions are affected by thoughts about 'submission rates' and 'blacklisting'. Does focus on submission adversely affect quality or is quality improved by thoughts of having to complete to clearly defined deadlines?

It was found that an important way in which students were helped to improve drafts of chapters was by encouragement to cut down the length of what they had written and to become more focused. There were a few supervisors in the sample who did not look at what their student had written until they had a complete draft of the thesis. But this minority approach to supervision of writing was limited to supervisors of part-time 'mature' students.

On the whole, supervisors read and commented on successive chapters as they were written. As students supplied them with drafts of chapters that they had seen before, the supervisors tended to become more insistent on getting their students to conform to increasingly rigorous standards. Students could also be expected to gain more time to complete by eventually having their thesis referred. Examiners in the sample mentioned theses that had one experiment or case study less then expected and a general incompleteness of some of the work that they were seeing:

> As an external, you are now often examining 'unfinished' theses and referral serves to give more time.

> The thesis may be over-ambitious and not quite 'cooked'.

It is not clear if re-submission rates are increasing but referral is perceived by some as a useful process which offers more feedback then would otherwise be available.

The few students who had already experienced a viva appreciated the opportunity of receiving very detailed feedback from the examiners. One of the two who had already completed believed most definitely that eventually his thesis was of a much higher standard than would otherwise have been the case.

People were asked what they thought they were doing when they were supervising, examining or working towards a PhD. Responses indicated that academics and students alike have difficulty in separating 'the PhD' from 'the thesis'; most used the terms synonymously. The closest to an actual definition of the PhD came from a member of staff: 'It's partly a piece of research and partly an examination.'

The students, as well as the staff, believed that a 'range' of possible standards existed. These had to do with such things as, for example, command of written English (foreign students):

> There's a tacit understanding that the standard is lower even though they are very diligent. It's not just the language, there's a tendency to limited critical awareness, more pedestrian, empirically based study without conceptual interest. No understanding of values and policy issues'. (Planning)

Concerning preparation for the oral examination, students seemed to appreciate that re-reading their completed thesis, as a whole, prior to the viva was 'illuminating' and 'quite different'.

Very few students had a mock viva or any other real preparation for the examination, apart from this reading-through of their theses. Although four of the supervisors did discuss what to expect, or even go through a mock viva, the majority of students did not even know the composition of their panel of examiners prior to the event. For example, of those students who had completed the first two years of registration, eleven did not have any idea how many examiners there would be or what their roles were and did not expect to know until the very last minute. The remaining thirteen had picked up something from former students about the time it takes, and of the atmosphere. Mostly the viva is a journey into the unknown. This lack of preparation was regardless of institution and seemed to depend on the practice of individual supervisors.

On the whole, then, it seems that students are not given sufficient information regarding what is required of them at earlier stages in the process. They are also ill-prepared for the viva when it occurs. While it is true that the final examination can be relatively unpredictable, it is still possible for the candidates to feel that they have had some practice for what they are to experience. Those students who *have* experienced a mock viva have taken it extremely seriously.

The viva as the final assessment of quality and standards

The research also involved a close perusal of the examination process itself. Knowledge of what happens here is important as it involves maintaining uniform standards of quality. Detailed accounts were collected from candidates and examiners regarding the process of the oral examination; what they considered the objectives to be; how they approached reaching these objectives and also some insight into their feelings about the whole experience.

A specific aspect of the process has to do with the selection of examiner. The interviews sought to discover what kinds of variations there are in the procedures employed. How much, if any, consultation involves the students and their suggestions concerning a suitable examiner, and what are the reasons for the choice that is made.

The viva is the ultimate test of quality that must be faced by students. The evaluation and maintenance of standards is the responsibility of those academics who are called upon to act as examiners. For these reasons the research sought to explore how and why certain people are selected to become examiners.

It was found that two of the institutions studied formally appointed PhD examiners through their centrally constituted graduate research committees. In these cases the committee looked to the supervisor for suggestions but the supervisor did not necessarily know which of the names suggested would be approached by the committee. One of the supervisors who had experienced this system said 'It's not clear precisely how they are chosen, if it is a precise procedure.'

In the other two institutions it was the responsibility of the supervisors to obtain the agreement of appropriate examiners for their students. In such cases the suggestions of the supervisor had to be ratified by a university-wide committee on the appointment of examiners. Here supervisors had different ideas of what criteria to use when making their choice. These included reputation, knowledge and sympathy to the subject, and, in some cases, sympathy to the student's approach. There was also a notion that they should be leaders in the field rather than people who were acquaintances of people known to the supervisor. One of the academics said:

> I'm against the practice of getting a lesser academic, or a friend,
> for a weaker student but I know it happens and it has happened
> here.

However, the primary reason for a committee not accepting the suggested academic was if his or her qualifications were not in the student's discipline. This could happen if, for example, the thesis was in the department of sociology but the topic had to do with health, or education. A supervisor might propose an examiner with medical or educational qualifications, or even a philosopher with appropriate knowledge and experience. However, the committee would be likely to insist on a sociologist unless a very good case could be made for the alternative.

Some supervisors thought it was preferable to have someone from within their own academic network. This was primarily because otherwise it was a 'stab in the dark'. This notion of a 'lottery' recurred although it was also thought that the whole thing was 'too cosy'. Some supervisors were critical of the system that they had experienced. One from an institution with a centrally located committee said:

> It's vital that they are *good* examiners. I've worked with some
> people who haven't read what they've been sent. Nor do I like
> examiners who have a particular view of life.

One, from an institution with a more personalised approach, thought that the system whereby the student and supervisor 'fix it up' could be improved. The suggestion was made that there should be a list of academics and their specialities available for reference. This would obviate the need for supervisors to 'phone people they did not know and ask what they worked on and whether they were willing to examine a particular thesis.

The question of student involvement in the choice of examiner was also explored. It was found that occasionally the student did have some idea of what was happening concerning the viva and/or the examination panel. In these cases the supervisor would have discussed possible examiners with the student. In other cases the supervisor neither consulted nor informed the student regarding which names were being put forward.

Experience of the examination

The interviews sought to establish what constitutes a 'typical' viva from the point of view of academics and those students who had already completed. The expectations of current research students were also explored. It was found that the viva can last from 45 minutes to 4 hours and can be anything from a friendly discussion to a detailed interrogation.

One examiner expressed the view that the viva:

> is a *rite de passage* and as such should not be enjoyed but reasonably traumatic, so that one may look back at 50 on how hard a time one was given.

It seems that this is not an unusual perception. The following quotation is taken from the interview of a part-time student who did her PhD while she was on the staff of the polytechnic:

> My viva was traumatic. I had to fight for my life. A very bad choice of examiners. Now I'm on the Faculty Board and the Degree Committee so that I see other externals' reports which include, at times, sadistic comments which I don't feel are suitable.

There were other examiners who were concerned that the viva was sometimes used to try and break the student's spirit and were concerned about the situation where the relationship is tied up with the examiner's own sense of worth:

> The problem with some academics is that they use whatever power they've got to demonstrate something about themselves.

> I'm concerned about the situation where the relationship is tied up with their own ego defence. Important to psychologically distance themselves.

The opinion was expressed by more than one of the supervisors that examiners need to show old-fashioned tolerance and attempt to think within the student's approach. 'Students do not need to be bruised in order to achieve high standards.' But, just as some supervisors had thought it important to select examiners who were sympathetic to the student's work, some examiners said that the most important thing was the need to be sympathetic to students during their oral examination.

However, although examiners differ in their ideas concerning the degree of formality or informality, enjoyment or anxiety that should be introduced into the viva, there is agreement between them as to what is expected with regard to standards. Presentation, or the physical appearance of the thesis itself, was considered by many to be disproportionately important. There was some agreement that if the document was expertly crafted using the latest word processing techniques then the initial reaction was a more favourable one than would be the case when first flicking through a less prepossessing document:

> I find it difficult to discipline myself against a beautifully pre-
> sented thesis versus the actual content. The visual impression of
> words on paper has a powerful effect on me.

Ratification of decisions

In three of the four institutions studied, each examiner is required to prepare a separate report prior to the viva. The report had to make a definite recommendation as to whether the thesis should be accepted for the degree but it is not necessary to submit the report until after the oral examination has been completed.

It was generally accepted that the examiners might confer as they are likely to know each other, but those members of staff who mentioned this did not think that it was common practice. After the examination has been conducted, the examiners report jointly and all the reports are submitted to the Degree Committee.

The Degree Committee requires explanations of any major discrepancies between individual and joint reports. If examiners disagree, the committee is empowered to overturn a report or appoint a third examiner to resolve the issue, but this is a rare occurrence.

The polytechnic was subject to CNAA regulations which differ slightly from university regulations in that the examiners' individual preliminary reports are required to be submitted prior to the oral examination. At the conclusion of the examination they submit their joint report, unless there is any disagreement in which case separate reports are submitted. (Although at the time of writing polytechnics have ceased to exist, it makes sense to report on procedures where they differed from the universities as there is no reason to assume that the new universities will change their practices as they change their names.)

Examiners must use their own discretion with regard to how they interpret the rather vague criteria provided by the examining institutions. This is likely to be related to their own belief regarding what the aim of PhD training is meant to be.[1] But, regardless of whether they believe that a PhD is training for a career in research or a preparation for the academic life, great emphasis is placed on the ability and experience of examiners in identifying truly outstanding work.

In fact, it was established that there is basic agreement concerning what examiners are looking for in a good candidate. They were happy to explain their interpretations of the criteria. These included considering how deeply the thesis goes into the issues and whether the student has faced up to everything involved; how they have dealt with contradictions in the evidence; and how they have sorted out, if not resolved, the problems. Examiners looked for conceptual understanding, critical ability and an explicit and well structured argument.

Examiners acknowledged that there were problems to do with nervousness and expressed the view that sometimes it is speed, rather than depth, of thought that is tested in such a context. They were also concerned about the problem of having to decide whether or not to penalise a candidate when it was really the academic who should be blamed for not having done the job of supervising properly.

Using the idea of undergraduate degree grades (2/2,2/1, etc.) as a guide that standards were not raised too high was a popular strategy to help decision making. By keeping these divisions as a yardstick in their mind, examiners were able to acknowledge that it was possible to gain a PhD for a piece of work that was less than 'excellent' although it was excellence that they were really looking for. The analogy to peer reviewing of journal articles was also popular:

> The standard of the PhD is measured by two 'wise' people which is similar to referees recommending to an editorial team whether articles are suitable for publication in a learned journal.

Whether examiners used mental yardsticks of undergraduate degrees or professional publications there was concern that 'a thesis may be "smuggled through" when there are still some questions over

---

1   Phillips and Pugh (1987) give several alternative aims held by examiners.

it'. There was mention of 'a lost consensus as to what makes good work.'

But still examiners requested re-submission, stating that it is not rare and may be due to unfinished work being presented because of the pressure for early submission. In all four institutions referral was now seen as normal by the staff, rather than being indicative of serious difficulties.

The suggestion was also made that the certificate awarded for the PhD should be more informative and should give some indication of the work that has been done. In addition to the fact that the candidate has gained the PhD, one examiner thought it important that the certificate should also include the title of the thesis.

The question still needs to be asked whether it is just the thesis that is being examined, or whether it is the candidate who is being assessed personally as someone who merits a doctorate or can be considered as an ambassador of the awarding institution.

Person or product?

When asked if the degree was given for the written product or the person who had emerged at the end of the system, examiners agreed that: 'Before the viva one can be persuaded that the text is of PhD quality' but indicated that if there was some discrepancy between the written words and the discussion during the examination the fact that the candidate was not as comfortable with the material as s/he was expected to be would disadvantage them.

Two of the examiners said that the degree is given to an individual but one of these modified this meaning by adding that this was 'only if both examiners recommended failure or re-submission' The other also had some reservations:

> if the words on the page are acceptable but the individual indicated during the course of the discussion that they were not really at home – that would count against them.

Of the remaining examiners, ten said that the PhD was awarded for written work only. A typical comment here was: We give it for the text unfortunately. But I do think we should have some other criteria too.' The other eleven said that the doctorate was awarded for both.

Students believe that the viva was to discover whether the thesis was 'any good' and that it was all their own work. Also it was seen as a forum for them to show the clarity of their thought and grasp of the work.

Increasingly supervisors may allow a low quality submission in order to accommodate deadlines and on the following two quotations taken from the interviews show, examiners feel hard pressed not to fail borderline theses:

> As an external, I've been badgered to pass the unpassable.

> It's very hard not to give the degree.

But where it was reported that comparison had been made with past theses, it was found that they were not better than present ones.

Statements from students about their experience after the oral examination has been completed lends credibility to the belief that there is very wide variation in conducting the viva. However, little or no information about what to expect is given to students prior to the event:

> I don't even know how many people will be there. I know they give you comments on your PhD and you may have to rewrite some of it. Nobody talks about it.

Much of what they believe happens during the examination is told to them, not by their supervisors, but by other research students:

> I spoke to other people about their vivas as they'd had them whilst I was a student.

> The only concrete information I have is from an acquaintance who's just completed and was talking about his viva.

There was also some confusion regarding what would happen, and therefore, what it was that they needed to prepare:

> I'm not sure what happens at the viva. I know that there will be a general discussion of the whole thesis. I've heard stories of enormously long PhDs and then someone criticises one significance level.

> I'm expecting something really tough; they try to take your work apart so that you can defend it. It can take hours and hours and we're all terrified.

As far as the examiners were concerned, it was found that there was some feeling that it was the supervisor who was being examined. One examiner expressed the problem like this:

> I judge it on the product and scratch my head and wonder about the supervisor. But I don't penalise someone for incompetent supervision.

In conclusion, it must be said that many examiners were not happy with the viva as it is at present although few could suggest a reasonable alternative.

'Not sure how I'd suggest modifying the viva but it's certainly a strange ritual' said one. While another supported the notion of a conference style report of work undertaken rather than a question

and answer session: 'I'd prefer the candidate to make a verbal presentation.'

Gender and its relationship to quality

Throughout the departments studied, there were many more male
academics than female (proportions varied between 10% and 30%).
When it came to senior staff and professors, the percentage of women
to men dropped dramatically.

Decision making is affected by these numbers as it is senior
committees that make policy and so women have little or no say in
policy issues. This is relevant to the issue of quality when we consider
what topics are thought to be worthy of serious research, which
methodological approaches are acceptable to investigate them, and
whether the theoretical frameworks which are employed to explain
the results are perceived as legitimate.

In one of the departments studied, it was agreed by all of those
interviewed, staff and students alike, that empirical research in their
field is primarily conducted by women while men do the theory
which carries higher status. In another department it was claimed
that there were some blatant, self-proclaimed 'misogynists'.

One student met considerable hostility from an 'anti-feminist
man' in the department. She reported that he wrote two pages of
'personal vitriol' on the paper that she had written for assessment
purposes and destroyed any confidence that she had had. She was
fortunate that her female supervisor tackled the committee with
regard to his abuse of power and the paper was passed at its first
reading. But this example demonstrates that validation from other
women is vital.

In fact gender relations impinged on issues of quality in a variety
of ways. Perhaps the most important, but least visible, of these had
to do with the research topic and methodology. One male supervisor
mentioned a thesis that he considered to be 'over-documented' in one
respect:

> She wrote a thesis on The Role of Women In Sumatra and gave 17
> references to show that women's role had not been considered.
> The problem in the thesis was that it didn't consider the role of
> men.

There are a number of areas of study that may be of interest to women
but hold little or no appeal for a male supervisor. Similarly, some
'feminist' methodologies or certain styles of reporting research are
more amenable to supervision by women. For example, one female
student said that the 'feminist approach is not considered as "real
work" to some men in the Faculty.' Another explained that:

Writing from a feminist perspective makes for difficulties as there are no feminists in permanent positions in the department.

Another female student, whose work involved questions of gender, commented that although as an undergraduate she had been taught 'there is no such thing as objectivity', she had discovered as a postgraduate that she and other women were criticised for not being objective in their research proposals. Yet, she argued:

> for feminists it's impossible to separate oneself from one's work. Writing oneself into the thesis and not being invisible is a gender issue.

While there are many satisfied women research students, the fact that there are more male than female members of academic staff available to supervise proportionately higher numbers of female students sometimes resulted in delays in student progress and depression with regard to their work. A male supervisor said: 'Women always moan no matter what time the courses are put on. I changed it to accommodate them and the same ones moaned again.' He was referring to the provision of a taught course component for research students. A female supervisor reported:

> In seminars it's primarily the men who speak; women are much less sure of the quality of their work which makes them needier and leads to their being more tentative in their writing.

A female student observed: 'You don't really realise it but the system is against you, there's so many men.' This male/female imbalance becomes important at the decision making level because, as one respondent put it:

> Only professors and senior committees are allowed to vote and we have 70 men professors to three women, resulting in policy decisions being out of the hands of women.

There is also the question of finding an examiner who believes that this is the kind of work that should be conducted. For example, quantitative work is very acceptable but 'new' areas concerning meaning and discourse are more controversial. In the department where there was disagreement about whether or not such an approach was acceptable, the debate resulted in a decision to set up a departmental 'Gender Sub-committee'.

With regard to supervision, a male academic with institutional responsibility for research students, said:

> Leaving aside the attitude of a very small number of my male colleagues who talk down to women in a way that they wouldn't to men students, women don't have any more problems than men do.

But finding the right supervisors for women students presents difficulties as there were either even numbers, or more female than male
research students in most of the departments studied. It is, therefore,
inevitable that many women students have male supervisors.

While this may work very well in many cases, there are also cases
where this pairing was perceived as the cause of specific problems;
for example, where the gender issue in research is not necessarily seen
as interesting by a male supervisor, or where there may be minor
interactional difficulties. As one female student who had two supervisors, one man and one woman, put it:

> It's different talking to a woman supervisor than a man. There's
> more of a bond between women. If something personal was
> disturbing me I wouldn't be able to talk to my male supervisor
> but I do to my female supervisor.

Another woman said: 'there's only one woman on the staff. She was
definitely a role model for me and my protection from male-female
power relationship. Without her I'd never have stayed.'

Conclusions

An important element in the whole of the research degree process is
to enable a student to come to the understanding that, in attaining a
PhD, brilliance is never a satisfactory substitute for perseverance.
But, as it is usually not until the end of their degree that students
discover that the thesis did not need magical qualities, that it was
merely a job of work that had to be completed, they are in an
ambiguous position for some considerable time. That is, they intend
to write the thesis 'some time in the future' but do not really believe
that they are capable of it. Hence the very large number of theses that
are not commenced until nearly all (or all) of the research is quite
finished. Chapman (1989) points out that evaluation is at the heart of
academic life and also that detailed information about assessment
criteria is rarely accessible to those being assessed.

This research showed that institutions do not always take advantage of the points where evaluation could be usefully employed and
that students are not as well informed of what is required as they
might be. In this regard, there is diversity of practice between different departments in the same institution and also between supervisors
in the same department.

Nevertheless, we must beware of the situation where discussions
of quality in higher education are replaced by discussions of assessment. The danger for the PhD, were this to happen, is that a coherent
whole may become less important than the individual sections of the

thesis. This is because a 'Literature Review' and 'Methodology Section', for example, can usually be evaluated against some external criteria such as relevant previous publications or traditionally acceptable approaches. The whole requires a more subjective mode of evaluation.

The various points, identified above, at which evaluation can occur – upgrading, monitoring work in progress, preparation for viva and the examination itself – are all points at which it is possible to encourage the development of high quality work. This can be done, at least in part, by ensuring that the environment within which the work is occurring is an appropriate environment. This would include reassessing the methods employed to decide whether and when upgrading from MPhil to PhD occurs, the way that information concerning different parts of the process of doing a research degree is imparted to students, and what it is that is being examined in the viva voce.

How selection is handled was included in the research because, provided the selection procedures are reliable, the risk of failure, drop-out or non-completion on time is minimised for both the institution and the students. Research requires different skills and abilities from those required in passing examinations for taught courses. What is needed is problem solving (and problem seeking) ability coupled with persistence. These differences should be borne in mind when determining selection procedures for research students and those procedures which affect the outcome should be carefully re-assessed. This re-assessment should be carried out by those currently involved in formulating strategies to improve standards in their departments and/or institutions. Such re-assessment must include the range of staff interests (where that determines selection), and consideration of the influence of funding and quota requirements. These need to be determined in a way that will optimise recruitment of students with the potential to succeed.

Where overseas students are accepted into a research degree course it is the responsibility of the institution, not the individual supervisor, to ensure that the student has access to language training resources which will facilitate an appropriate standard of written English for the thesis. Too many supervisors are currently involved in the moral conflict concerning the extent to which they should intervene in the writing process as the student comes to the end of his or her period of registration.

This problem arises when good students have difficulty expressing themselves in writing. Such difficulties often arise because overseas applicants were accepted into the system without the extent of the language requirements for the finished thesis being made known to them. It cannot be stressed too strongly that writing, and help with writing, must start very early and continue throughout the period of registration.

It is possible to use the upgrading process as an opportunity to teach and prepare the student for what is required. But not all institutions take advantage of this opportunity.

Currently, there is a range of different procedures in operation and, depending on what has happened at the point of upgrading students can:

(a) remain completely unconscious of having to accomplish anything other than an acceptable thesis at the end of three or four years; or

(b) become extremely anxious about whether or not they will be upgraded.

The anxiety may be due either to the expected procedure or the uncertainty of how they can ever achieve the required standard, since they do not know what it is or how upgrading is decided. It is essential that a formalised procedure for upgrading is agreed by academic staff and made explicit to students at an early point in their period of registration.

How annual report forms are handled (especially when these are the only method of monitoring progress) also needs to be formalised. These forms, properly processed, can be of enormous value both to the student and to the institution. Unfortunately, there are some departments where the forms are completed and then filed away rather than being used for information purposes by relevant staff and feedback for the students.

Such forms should be agreed in consultation with student representatives. They should be kept as simple as possible and training or, at least, guidelines on their completion should be given to all supervisors. For the system to work some kind of assurance has to be built in to the effect that it is not the supervisor who is being assessed, although some element of supervisor assessment will be unavoidable.

The students, who are after all the other party to all this, are not usually given very much information about what is actually required of them or what to expect in the oral examination. (Some supervisors do arrange a mock viva but this is not general practice at present.) I would suggest that one of the final tasks of the supervisor should be either to give, or arrange for a colleague to give, a mock viva to the candidate. Apart from the obvious benefits of discussing their work and having the opportunity to see where they might have to reformulate some of their ideas, they also have the advantage that comes from revising for any examination.

The research results also showed that there is variation in both the experience that students have of the examinations and the methods by which examiners are selected.

With regard to the final examination, it appears that very little has changed in the years since I noted that the viva itself can range from being experienced as a pleasant after-tea chat, to a persecutory inquisition (Phillips 1985). Within the context of quality it would now seem to be appropriate that some kind of formulation be adopted that made such extremes less likely to occur.

Quality in the PhD is determined by the examiners but the standard has never been satisfactorily defined. The way in which their decisions are ratified were similar in the university sector but a little different in the polytechnic.

Overall, this research revealed that, while there is basic agreement between examiners regarding what it is that they are looking for, most students are given insufficient information regarding what is required of them. Finally, it was found that gender issues did affect the outcome of the work in certain cases where there was some controversy over the research topic, methodology or style of reporting results.

In conclusion, it is clear that not only do customs vary in important ways between institutions, but there are also differences between social science departments in the same institution. This is not surprising given the range of disciplines encompassed by 'social science' and the variation of institutional policies with regard to research students.

However, although the problems may be dependent upon particular methodologies and theoretical approaches, the possibility of maintaining contact with and knowledge of any given project during the course of the student's registration for a research degree is potentially the same for all departments if the suggestions made here with regard to assessing quality at different points during the period of registration are put into operation.

If supervisors, and their employing institutions, do adopt such suggestions, at least on a trial basis, they will almost certainly raise the probability of successful completion of high quality PhDs. As an added bonus they will also find that they have a more confident and less stressed population of postgraduate research students.

Acknowledgement

The support of the Economic and Social Research Council (ESRC) is gratefully acknowledged. The work described is part of the Research into Training Program supported by the Postgraduate Training Board, award number T007 40 1008. Any views expressed, however, are those of the author and do not necessarily reflect those of the ESRC.

References

Chapman, A.J. (1989) *Assessing research: citation-count shortcomings. The Psychologist 8*, 336–344.

CVCP (1991) *Teaching Standards and Excellence in Higher Education: Developing a Culture for Quality.* Occasional Green Paper No 1.

Government White Paper on Education (1991).

Hudson, L. (1960) Degree class and attainment in scientific research'. *British Journal of Psychology 51*, 1, 67–73.

Hudson, L. (1977) Picking winners: a case study in the recruitment of research students. *New Universities Quarterly 32*, 1, 88–107.

Miller, G.W. (1970) *Success, Failure and Wastage in Higher Education.* London: University of London Institute of Education/Harrap.

Phillips, E.M. (1985) Supervising postgraduates at a distance. *Teaching at a Distance 26*, 23–31.

Phillips, E.M. (1991) Learning to do research. In N.C. Smith and P. Dainty (eds) *The Management Research Handbook.* London: Routledge.

Phillips, E.M. (1992) The Concept of Quality in the PhD. In D. Cullen (ed) *Proceedings of the Conference on Quality in PhD Education.* Canberra: Australian National University.

Phillips, E.M. and Pugh, D.S. (1987) *How to Get a PhD: Managing the Peaks and Troughs of Research.* Milton Keynes: Open University Press.

Pirsig, R.M. (1976) *Zen and the Art of Motor Cycle Maintenance.* London: Corgi Books.

Part III

Completion and Employment

Chapter 8

Social Science Research Degrees
Completion Times and Rates

David Dunkerley and Jeffrey Weeks

Introduction

ESRC's 'Research Into Training' Programme has been the most systematic and thorough attempt in the UK to investigate a wide range of issues and concerns surrounding completion rates and times. The research upon which this chapter is based has been part of the Programme and reports on the first study to obtain a national database on social science research degree candidates that subsequently allows for an analysis of a wide range of variables that might affect the success of candidates.

It is somewhat surprising how few previous studies have been undertaken on the study of completion rates and times and their relation to a range of variables such as academic discipline, qualifications, age, mode of study and gender. Possibly the most comprehensive is Rudd and Hatch's (1968) study of postgraduate education, although it is extremely dated. The study's cohort comprised all students starting their postgraduate studies in 1957. From the 2200 responses, the study reported an overall wastage rate of 22 per cent. Included was significant variation with a 15 per cent wastage rate in science, whilst arts subjects reported a 50 per cent wastage. Given that the data are now over thirty years old, the contemporary relevance of the findings is questionable.

It would appear that the completion rates in arts and social science disciplines are significantly lower than for science and technology disciplines. Indeed, there is less likelihood of completion at all in the former disciplines. Furthermore, full-time candidates seem more likely to complete than part-time candidates (Phillips 1980, Phillips and Pugh 1987, Wilkinson 1989). And again, there is some evidence to suggest that older candidates (Wright and Lodwick 1989) and women candidates (Rudd 1990) have lower completion rates.

Background

During its 28-year life (1964–92) the Council for National Academic Awards (CNAA) was the chartered body with responsibility for awarding degrees in polytechnics and colleges throughout the United Kingdom, offering a range of qualifications from certificates and diplomas through first degrees and master's programmes to research degrees at MPhil and PhD levels. It was a unique national body working closely with over 200 polytechnics, colleges and institutes of higher education as well as, in the field of research degrees, with a host of other organisations such as industrial concerns and research institutes.

During its lifetime, over 16000 students were registered for research degrees with the CNAA, with over 6000 conferments of awards. Inevitably, given the origins of the polytechnics and many of the colleges in technological institutions, the majority of these awards have been in areas of science and technology. Increasingly, however, there was a growing number of registrations in other areas, especially the social sciences, reflecting the continuing expansion and diversification of teaching in the polytechnic and college sector of higher education.

Although students were recruited individually by the polytechnics and colleges, or other sponsoring establishments, and the studies were supervised and administered in these institutions, CNAA as the ultimate degree awarding body required that all relevant information regarding the programme of studies, supervision and all other matters relating to a student's progression was lodged with the Council. As a consequence, CNAA had full records of all these registrations, together with considerable administrative information about the various stages of the research student's work up to completion and submission, and conferment details. This provides an incomparable archive, which has provided the data for this research.

This administrative system is of more than historical interest since most of the new universities established in 1992 have adopted variants of the CNAA model in their new research degree regulations. They have recognised the value of the regulations in ensuring and maintaining quality whilst at the same time protecting the interests of the candidate.

Methodology

Information source

We were aware from our different involvements in the CNAA (one a 'member', the other an 'officer') of the existence of very detailed information on research degree candidates stretching back over twenty years covering the 'public sector' of higher education (i.e. the non-university sector as defined prior to 1989) held by the Council. Having obtained permission to gain access to this information, the aim of the study was to create a database relating to research degree candidates in the social sciences registered with the CNAA that would provide the opportunity for a quantitative study using historical and contemporary data. Since the wide range of variables available were largely compatible with those employed by the ESRC, it was possible to undertake a systematic study using these data in order to explore relationships of the variables to ultimate completion rate and time status.

The data were derived entirely from information held on the relevant CNAA forms submitted by sponsoring establishments; since these forms had to be used in all cases an initial consistency could be assumed as to the type of information available. The form changed slightly over the years but not sufficiently as to prevent comparable data being extracted over different time periods. The majority of the information concerning candidates was contained in the initial registration form since it was here that personal details about the candidate, the quality of the supervisory team, information about collaboration, the level of funding and available facilities for the project were given. All this was in addition to a very full statement about the objectives, methods and projected progress of the research study.

There was a variety of other forms used during the career of a CNAA research degree candidate. For those candidates transferring from MPhil to PhD a special transfer form existed where both the candidate and supervisors commented on the suitability of the project for such transfer and a summary of progress with the main project and the programme of related studies was made. Other forms gave details of the examination arrangements and examination outcomes, whether (and why) a change in supervisors was made and whether a change in mode of study had occurred (normally from full-time to part-time). A form did not exist to cover a request for a suspension of registration but the relevant information was available in a detailed letter from the sponsoring establishment.

It is clear from the above that most of the information was available as responses to highly structured questions; interpretation of responses was unnecessary. Where there were open-ended questions requiring interpretation the problem was one of creating appropriate categories. No pilot study in the traditional sense of the term could be undertaken; instead the categories were derived from taking a 2.5 per cent pilot of responses, analysing these and then deciding on the categories.

Defining the sample

The data from the Research Councils on completion rates have, to an extent, a fundamental problem with the operational definition employed. The definition of success is normally that of submitting a PhD thesis within four years of registration. The problem is that if a student submits in four and a half years or possibly is awarded an MPhil, he/she by this definition is not successful. The definition also neglects the fact that the research training acquired by a postgraduate student, whilst not necessarily leading to a successful degree outcome, can be of immeasurable value in a subsequent career that rates success in terms of expertise rather than formal qualifications.

The definition of what subjects comprise social science differed between the CNAA and ESRC. Obviously, data presented on the forms reflected CNAA's definition. This required, in some cases, some re-definition in line with the ESRC definition in order that data might, in due course, be compared with other studies in the ESRC research programme. In fact, the revised definition arrived at was a combination of the CNAA and ESRC lists – the latter being that used since October 1988 for ESRC studentship competitions; the former was the CNAA conferment list employed from 1987.

A further task in defining the sample, having overcome the definitional problems, was the actual selection of candidates to be included. Where registrations had been completed (or terminated) no problem arose – all candidates who had their degrees conferred together with those who had withdrawn or failed within the defined subject areas were selected for inclusion in the total sample. For those students who were currently registered, a problem arose. It was not worth analysing those who had only recently registered, for this would contribute nothing to achieving the aims of the study. It was therefore decided, since the major aim of the study was to analyse completion rates and completion times, to select all the current candidates who on 1 March 1990 should have completed their studies and submitted their theses if notional completion times were employed.

For the purposes of this study, submission times and completion times are treated as interchangeable categories. In practice, the former refers to the time at which a thesis is submitted for examination and is the date employed by the ESRC for purposes of calculating whether a thesis is on time or not; the latter is the period after which the examination process is completed and a decision made about the award. Throughout, when the term 'completion' is employed, the actual period referred to is that between registration and submission in order that comparison may be made with ESRC data.

Results

The 1969 cases comprising the CNAA sample are listed in Table 8.1 by subject area (it should be noted that the classification in the table is by CNAA Committee rather than by individual discipline, although certain disciplines are readily identifiable such as Geography, Economics and Sociology). The asterisked disciplines are those where a judgement had to be made as to whether a project might properly be regarded as a social science one.

Over the whole period, male students were heavily over-represented, comprising 63 per cent of the total, but the proportion of female candidates had increased from a mere 20 per cent in 1966 to virtually a half of all registrations by 1989.

The age distribution of the sample is interesting, showing a virtual 50–50 split between candidates who, at the time of registration, were aged 30 years or under and those aged over 30 years. Analysis has shown that older students were more likely to be registered as part-time candidates.

In terms of qualifications, a quarter (470) possessed a UK master's degree at the time of registration. The CNAA regulations allowed for registration for PhD direct if the master's degree is deemed to be relevant, suggesting that over three-quarters of the sample would not have been able to take this route but would have had to register for either MPhil only or for MPhil with transfer possibility to PhD. In fact, only 12 per cent (234 individuals) of the total registered for PhD direct, whereas 51 per cent (1003) took the route of MPhil with transfer possibility with the remaining registering for MPhil only.

The above suggests that the 'normal' entrant would be an individual with a first degree only. The CNAA regulations defined a 'normal' candidate as one with a UK first or second-class honours degree; there are, however, provisions for 'non-standard' entry including degree qualifications below a second, overseas qualifications, professional qualifications and so on. In spite of the flexibility of the regulations, only 124 candidates were registered with less than a second-class honours degree. The modal qualification, as might be expected, was an upper second and accounted for half of candidates possessing UK

**Table 8.1: CNAA Research degree candidates
by subject area 1970–90**

Subject	Number in sample	%
Education	451	22.9
Business and Management Studies	356	18.1
Sociology	268	13.6
Economics	142	7.2
History*	124	6.3
Legal Studies	110	5.6
Psychology*	75	3.8
Public and Social Administration	75	3.8
Health and Medical Studies	67	3.4
Town Planning	65	3.3
Politics	55	2.8
Geography*	47	2.4
Architecture*	47	2.4
Library Studies	24	1.2
Food and Retail Studies	18	0.9
Linguistics*	8	0.4
Environmental Studies*	2	0.1
Other	35	1.8
Total	**1969**	**100**

degrees. More frequently were those individuals with a professional qualification (134). Only 113 candidates had overseas qualifications.

One feature of CNAA research degree candidates that often differed from their university counterparts is the fact that their research was often undertaken in conjunction with a collaborating establishment. The Council actively encouraged such collaboration where the possibility existed for it to be real and meaningful. Many social science projects, of course, are not amenable to such collaboration and yet over a half (53.2%) of the sample had such collaboration. The form this collaboration took varied but 41 per cent were provided with access for their empirical work, 29 per cent were given advice on their projects and 25 per cent were using their work-places for the purposes of collaboration. This might partly explain why only 8 per cent of the total were in collaboration with an industrial or commercial organisation.

A high percentage (42%) were not in receipt of any funding for their studies and less than a half (48%) received regular funding from any source. In part, this is explained by the fact that over a half of candidates (64%) were registered as part-time students for the duration of their studies. Seventy-eight per cent of the part-time candidates were self-funded. It is the case that some transfer from full-time to part-time status occurred, largely as a result of the cessation of funding and the programme of work not having been completed. In fact 13 per cent of the total sample changed their mode of study in this way.

The vast majority of funded candidates, at the time of initial registration, were employed by or funded by public sector organisations; only 8 per cent of the total were employed in the private sector. This high public sector profile is partly explained by the fact that the polytechnics and colleges, whilst under the control of local education authorities, were often generous in providing funding for research degree candidates as research assistants. Furthermore, it is probably in the nature of social science projects that they should emanate from and be related to the public sector. It is interesting to note that the small number of candidates from the private sector were predominantly registered as part-time candidates (85%).

The database also provides some interesting descriptive figures on candidates' supervisors and examiners. The CNAA regulations stipulated that a candidate must have at least two supervisors, one of whom was designated as the Director of Studies. With regard to the latter, 60 per cent themselves had a PhD and almost a third had a master's degree. Although 60 per cent of them were on the lecturer career scale, it is interesting to note that a quarter had Head of Department status. What is surprising is that 45 per cent of the Directors of Studies had not previously supervised to completion and a third were not supervising any other candidates and so were supervising only one candidate. The figures show that overall the second supervisor was not as well qualified as the first and more were on the lecturer scale. This suggests that in many cases the role of second supervisor was often one of 'apprentice'.

Another feature of the CNAA system was that of the Programme of Related Studies. The aim was that a training element was built into the research programme. The majority of candidates (71%) took the opportunity of attending seminars and/or lectures; 10 per cent attended whole courses; and 19 per cent undertook a course of guided reading.

Before getting to the stage of submission (assuming there had not already been a withdrawal) 22 per cent of the candidates requested an extension to their period of registration, the main reasons being employment or domestic problems (43%), problems with the research itself (27%), a change of employment (16%) and medical reasons (8%).

Outcomes of registration

Taking the total sample of 1969 candidates, 39 per cent (795) had their award conferred, less than 1 per cent had failed, 14 per cent of the registrations were still current. This left a staggering 46 per cent of the total or 910 candidates who had withdrawn their registrations. This very high withdrawal rate is examined in more detail below.

When candidates did actually submit their theses, the prognosis was good. Fewer than 2 per cent failed, 11.5 per cent were invited to submit, 32 per cent had to make only minor amendments and 55 per cent passed first time without amendments. Thus, nearly 90 per cent of those submitting were given a first-time pass or had to make only a slight amendment to their thesis.

Missing data only allows 648 of the 759 cases of conferments to be looked at in terms of the time taken to complete the degree. Overall, using the ESRC criterion of a submission within four years, 39.5 per cent completed on time (thus, 60.5% were late). A potential problem in interpreting this figure is that many of the candidates registering with the CNAA – most especially part-time and/or self-funded candidates – might not have perceived themselves as working towards the kind of deadline suggested by the ESRC. Many CNAA candidates had as their aim the completion of their degree *per se* rather than to finish in a set period of time. Such a suggestion is reinforced by the fact that 67.5 per cent of candidates completed within a year of the recommended times. It is reasonable to assume that candidates' perceptions of completion times are related to their mode of study, their funding source and the type of degree for which they are registered. Indeed, these three variables were found to be of the greatest influence. Of course, the three variables are themselves related insofar as part-time candidates are more likely to be funding themselves and registering for an MPhil rather than a PhD. This, in turn, relates to candidates' own goals regarding completing on or over time as suggested above.

Of the 648 candidates whose mode of study and completion time is known, 37 per cent studied full-time, 52 per cent studied part-time and 11 per cent changed their mode of study from full to part-time. When mode of study is cross-tabulated with whether 'on time' or not an interesting pattern emerges. The most successful candidates, in terms of completing on time, were those registered in the part-time mode; the least successful (20%) were those who changed their mode of study. The very poor results for the 'changed' group arises from the fact that in changing the normal reason was the cessation of funding. So when this group changes to a part-time mode they are already approaching an over-run of the allowed time period. Although the percentage completing within one year more than doubles from the 'on-time' category it is still low and possibly reflects the demands of new commitments arising, particularly, from employment.

Turning to degree type at this stage of registration, PhD candidates more generally are full-time and yet full-timers have a poorer completion time. But PhD direct students have much better completion times, showing again the complexity of this situation. This apparent paradox is developed further below.

The third variable – extent of funding – reflects the results for the mode of study as seen below. So the relationship between mode of study and funding is far stronger than degree type is to cither mode or funding level. There are very similar completion times for those with no funding (46% on time) and part-time candidates (48%). Those who are fully funded and those who are full-time have exactly the same percentage submitting on time.

The analysis of funding proved interesting since it showed that those with partial funding proved to be the best performers (albeit only marginally better than those with no funding). It must be a matter of concern that those with full-funding have the worst performance rate in terms of completion on time. This is the opposite of what, *a priori*, may have been assumed.

Factors affecting outcomes

Subject differences

Of the six largest disciplines represented in the sample (i.e. those with over 100 candidates and representing three-quarters of all candidates), the most successful groups are the more vocationally-orientated ones – business and management studies, education and economics – where there tends to be a higher proportion of part-time candidates reading for MPhil degrees. In education, for example, 20 per cent of all candidates were registered for an MPhil only. Sociology had the poorest performance in terms of conferment (31%) and the highest withdrawal rate (54%). It has already been established that MPhil candidates are more likely to complete so if a subject has a higher proportion of MPhil-only registrations a higher overall conferment might be expected anyway.

When time taken by subject area is examined, economics has the most successful rate (58% on time), followed by education (48%), history (38%), business and management studies (36%), sociology (35%) and legal studies (31%).

Gender

Little difference was found between the performance of men and women; in fact, outcomes are remarkably similar. Exactly the same percentage withdrew (46%). For those currently registered there is only a 2.6 per cent difference in favour of women. The major difference between the two lies in whether they complete on time. Here males have a better performance with 44 per cent compared to the female completion rate on time of 32 per cent.

Age

The conferment rate for those aged 30 or under is higher than for the older group (54% compared with 46%). Fifty-nine per cent of the PhDs conferred were to the younger group. This finding can be related to Wright and Lodwick's (1989) conclusion that in the first year of study the more chronologically mature student makes better progress than the younger candidate. The better overall performance of the latter in the present study may be related to a range of other variables such as mode of study, pressure of other commitments and general motivation. The withdrawal rate is virtually identical. Interestingly, if one looks at current registrations, 64 per cent are in the younger group and 71 per cent of the full-time registrations were also in the younger group.

Degree type

The best conferment rate is to be found amongst candidates who register for and submit an MPhil (42%), followed by the PhD direct registration (39%), whilst those obtaining a PhD via an initial MPhil registration have a conferment figure of 36 per cent. The PhD direct category has the highest withdrawal rate of 49 per cent, the lowest being MPhil where only 43 per cent withdrew.

Mode of study

Taking mode of study at registration, the conferment rate does not differ very much between full-time candidates (41%) and part-time candidates (36%). There is more of a difference in the withdrawal rate (full-time 41%, part-time 51%). Of the total part time registrations (excluding withdrawals and current registrations) only 11 per cent of candidates were awarded a PhD compared to 20 per cent of the full-time candidates.

Qualifications

As might be expected, the proportion of PhDs awarded increases with the level of qualification at registration as does generally the overall conferment rate. Thus 42 per cent of those candidates with first-class honours in the sample had their research degree conferred (approximately half of them being PhDs), dropping to 36 per cent for those with lower seconds. This pattern is consistent with that found by Rudd (1990). In the non-standard entry category, only a quarter of those with third-class degrees completed. A similar pattern emerges with withdrawal rates with 63 per cent of those without an honours degree withdrawing compared with 39 per cent of those with a first. The possession of a relevant Master's degree did not seem to improve the conferment rate; in fact, at 34 per cent it is worse than for those candidates with a lower second class honours degree. In Geography, Whitehand (1966) also showed the creditable performance of candidates possessing a lower class of degree than an upper second.

Turning to those candidates registered with non-standard qualifications not already discussed, the conferment rates compare very favourably with those possessing UK degrees: 59 per cent of those with foreign BAs; 45 per cent of those with sub-degree qualifications (e.g. HND); and 38 per cent of those with professional qualifications such as a CQSW or PGCE had their degrees awarded. Further analysis showed that those with a foreign BA were most likely to be studying full-time (76%) whilst the professionally qualified and sub-degree candidates were more likely to be on the part-time route (77% and 81% respectively).

No consistent pattern could be discerned when analysing the relationship between qualifications and completing on time. For example, those with first-class honours had the same percentage (41%) completing on time as those with third-class honours; those with a master's degree completed on time at the same rate as non-honours degree candidates (45%).

Data also exist on the performance of candidates according to how long a gap existed between completing previous studies and embarking on work for a higher degree. Two quite distinct patterns were established. There is a greater chance of having a research degree conferred the less time there is between last and present study. Thus, for those moving straight from under-graduate to postgraduate work the conferment rate is 42.5 per cent dropping to 35.1 per cent for those having a gap of between 10 and 15 years. This is to be expected because of the close relationship here to the age of the candidate. Yet when it comes to completion time, the figures for these two groups are 66 per cent and 49 per cent over time respectively. With both trends, the intermediate years show this consistent pattern.

Supervision

The CNAA regulations specified that each candidate must have at least two supervisors, one of whom was designated as the Director of Studies. Very few candidates had more than two supervisors so this category will be ignored in this analysis. Taking supervisors' academic qualifications, Director of Studies with no more than a first degree had students with a lower conferment rate – 36 per cent compared with 40 per cent with a postgraduate degree. The withdrawal rate of these students was also higher (52% compared with 45%). In the case of second supervisors the results showed no consistency whatsoever. It has suggested that the lack of experience of supervision amongst former polytechnic and college staff constitutes a problem not encountered as widely in the older universities. This has undoubtedly been the case in earlier years although the 'master/apprentice' approach to supervision insisted on by the CNAA was a useful way of over-coming the difficulty.

The post held by supervisors at the time that candidates registered also reveals some interesting findings. Readers are the most successful in getting their students to pass their degrees – 43.5 per cent of candidates whose Director of Studies or second supervisor was a Reader had their degree conferred. Heads of Department were the next most successful group followed by those on the lecturer scale. One interesting observation is the high conferment of 48 per cent when the second supervisor is a non-academic. This could be a vindication of CNAA's policy of encouraging external collaboration.

No consistent pattern could be identified when looking at candidates' success and the number of other candidates supervisors were supervising. Similarly, no pattern could be established when looking at the numbers of previous successful supervisions.

Funding

When sources of funding and outcomes are examined, the highest conferment rate is for those with overseas funding (52%), reflecting the results of those with overseas qualifications where there is probably high motivation, full funding and full-time study. It is also worth noting that the conferment rate for both ESRC (albeit with small numbers overall) and LEA funded candidates (39% and 40% respectively) is not much better than that for self-funded students (37%), although the latter do not have a much higher withdrawal rate.

As far as completion times and funding source is concerned, again the overseas candidates top the league with 52 per cent completing on time. The next best groups are the self-funded candidates (45%), ESRC (42%) and public bodies (40%) down to the LEA group (30%). This low percentage for LEA funded candidates is, in all probability, related to cessation of funding and the specific posts.

Withdrawal analysis

The high withdrawal rate discovered amongst the overall sample (46% or 910 candidates out of a total of 1969) warrants a separate analysis in order to discover whether there appear to be specific indicators suggesting a greater propensity to withdraw. In the majority of cases, broad reasons for withdrawing are available. It is worth highlighting that a mere ten candidates withdrew for financial reasons. Taking the variables examined above when discussing conferment rates and completion rates and times, a number of points emerge. **Gender** appears not to be a factor in withdrawal since of the total withdrawal cohort 36.7 per cent were female, 63.3 per cent male – this distribution corresponds exactly to the overall gender balance of the total sample. With regard to **age**, half of the withdrawals were 30 or under – again, this is roughly the same as for those passing, failing or current. It would appear, then, that like gender, age does not affect withdrawal.

The **discipline groups** show a variation of around 11 per cent. Taking the largest subject groups, the degree type originally registered does not explain the differences. For example, although sociology has a lower MPhil-only registration rate, this is also true of economics where the withdrawal rate is that much lower.

Turning to **degree type**, PhD direct has the highest withdrawal rate (49.1%), followed by MPhil/PhD with 47.9 per cent and MPhil only having 43 per cent withdrawal. Again, breaking these figures down further, in order to ascertain when candidates withdraw, the same percentage withdraw by the time they reach their allowed time periods for both MPhil and PhD registrations; in the case of full-time candidates a third did so, for full-timers two thirds of the MPhil and three-quarters of the PhD candidates had done so.

Although, as seen above, financial factors were rarely cited as a reason for withdrawing, the **extent of funding** does seem to play a part. Of those with no funding 51.5 per cent withdrew, compared with 41.3 per cent with full funding 46.4 per cent with partial funding. This pattern is reinforced when the funding source is examined since the self-funded group have the highest withdrawal rate (51.1%).

ESRC funded students have the second highest rate of withdrawal (44.7%). The data available do not allow an analysis of the effect of the ESRC sanctions policy since 1985 but there is evidence of the rate dropping for ESRC funded students. Thus, of the 51 students who withdrew in this category, 39 per cent withdrew between 1977–79, 21 per cent between 1980–82 and 19 per cent between 1983–85.

As might be expected, the **mode of study** seems to be related to withdrawal rates with 39 per cent of the full-timers and 51 per cent of the part-timers withdrawing. A similar expected pattern is found when **qualifications** are examined. Thus, for those with UK first degrees there is a direct relationship so that the lowest rate of withdrawal is amongst those with first-class honours (39%) and the highest in the non-honours degree category (63%). The best figure (i.e. lowest withdrawal rate) is found amongst those with a foreign BA (30%). A curious relationship is found when the influence of a UK master's degree is analysed, for such candidates have a higher withdrawal rate (52%) than those who did not possess a UK master's degree and withdrew (44%). The reasons given for withdrawal correspond to those for the sample as a whole and the funding level is also not a factor.

Conclusions and implications

The research upon which this chapter is based has been the first attempt to collate and analyse national data relating to research degrees in the social sciences. It is far from being a complete picture of the process involved in the acquisition of a research degree in that the data are highly quantitative. In a sense, they have to speak for themselves. It would be unrealistic to bring too much interpretation into any conclusions since the study has not allowed for the introduction of qualitative material. However, other studies forming part of ESRC's Research into Training Programme reported in this volume have used a more qualitative approach to their topics and thereby complement the material presented here.

What the study has been able to achieve is a systematic analysis of a wide range of quantitative variables and their apparent effect on completion outcomes and completion times. This, in itself, has certain hazards associated with it. For example, the notion of expected completion time may be artificial and dictated by funding bodies. The vast majority of the candidates comprising this sample were not under pressure from such funding bodies, very many of them were part-time candidates working at their own pace, using their own money and doing the work for their own interest and motives. Whilst it might be certain to assume that, at the outset, the motivation was there to complete, it is far more problematic to assume that such candidates were undertaking their work with a time-limited pressure upon them.

Equally, whilst grant-awarding bodies might regard a non-submission within a predefined time as unacceptable, many of the candidates included in this sample would regard themselves as successful by the mere fact of submission (and passing) no matter how long the work took.

There is a related issue in that the high withdrawal rate identified does not necessarily indicate that the work undertaken, but not completed, has been wasted. The research training element of a research degree has a lasting value that does not necessarily lead to the award of a research degree *per se*. Examples abound of individuals who have not completed their theses but who, as a result of the research skills acquired whilst candidates, now hold senior research positions in both public and private sector organisations.

The data discussed in this chapter are unique; they are also specific to what was until 1992 a particular sector of higher education in the UK. This sector had lagged somewhat behind the traditional university sector both in the growth of social science itself and, more especially, in its research degree work. That position has changed very considerably particularly in the last ten years and is far from being static.

The findings confirm various assumptions made about the performance of social science research degree candidates; at other times they have brought to light dramatic issues not previously considered; at other times still, there have been curious relationships suggested that are not readily explainable especially with the quantitative data available. In no particular order of priority these issues can be highlighted and distinguished as being of particular note for further discussion, reflection and investigation:

- CNAA candidates have a very high withdrawal rate. To an extent this was to be expected given the high proportion of part-time candidates with little or no funding, demands of other commitments and sustaining a long-term commitment. The actual extent of withdrawal is, however, surprising and raises questions about the selection of such candidates in the first place. Should postgraduate admissions tutors be more rigorous in their selection process; prior to registration should such candidates complete, for example, a course in research training to

ensure that they are capable of completing the proposed
work; should supervision of such candidates be more
systematic; should greater efforts be made to integrate
part-time candidates into the postgraduate community?

However, it is not only the part-time candidates who withdrew
in large numbers. Many of the full-time ones do not complete.
The study has shown the variations according to a range of
variables such as discipline and supervision; what has not been
possible has been an analysis of qualitative indicators such as
the research environment or the research ethos of particular
departments. Postgraduate research is always a lonely activity
but it may be that many of the full-time candidates have been
working in departments where a very small number of such
individuals were also working. The CNAA database does not
allow an investigation of such an issue, but additional work
might prove how important this is.

- It has been interesting to note the popularity of the MPhil
  degree as a final qualification in this sector. A higher
  proportion of MPhil candidates in certain areas seems to be
  related to part-time candidature, to studies that might be
  more work-related and applied in nature. This is slight
  conjecture but the study has demonstrated that the MPhil
  degree is perceived as worthwhile in its own right and a
  valuable qualification. Too often, it has been perceived as a
  consolation to a failed doctorate.

- Basic demographic indicators such as age and gender do not
  appear to affect outcomes to any large degree. The
  performance of males and females was shown to be
  remarkably similar whilst only marginal variations were
  found between younger and older cohorts. The latter is, if
  anything, slightly surprising since it might be expected that
  older candidates would have a range of external
  commitments and pressures not experienced by younger
  ones and, indeed, that the former might be more likely to be
  part-time registrations.

- The relatively poor performance of candidates already
  possessing a master's degree is difficult to explain,
  especially since it might be assumed that a taught master's
  degree would include, in many cases, a significant
  methodological component that could prove useful at the
  research stage and facilitate a more successful outcome.

- CNAA's policy of allowing applicants with non-standard qualifications to register for a research degree is vindicated to a degree. It is understood that such candidates present a risk in terms of non-completion or late-completion. The fact that so many do successfully complete is worth noting especially since such candidates are unlikely to be in receipt of funding. Of course, this very fact might provide for greater personal motivation.

- The quality of the supervision does seem to be an important issue, for the data show that the more experienced supervisor and the supervisor who has designation of research manager (such as a Reader) appears to achieve better results than the supervisor who is more specifically a member of the teaching staff. The requirement in the CNAA regulations for there to be more than one supervisor was perhaps one that could be emulated elsewhere since it affords the opportunity (and indeed the requirement) of previous successful supervisory experience.

- The low conferment rate overall is disappointing but even more so for those candidates who are fully-funded for a three year full-time period such as ESRC students. The fact that over the 20-year period covered by the research the conferment rate for the latter was only slightly better than that for self-funded students is a matter of concern.

- CNAA regulations always insisted on a programme of related studies for research degree candidates. In many respects this programme comprised systematic research training for candidates in that attendance at specialist courses and conferences were normally central features. The CNAA database, in itself, does not enable an analysis of whether such a programme enhances the possibility of completion but it is worth noting that the ESRC, in its 1991 Guidelines, now insists on a structured programme of training.

- There is no doubt that considerable benefits are derived from programmes of research undertaken with a collaborating establishment. The CNAA always encouraged this kind of arrangement and clearly, from the data presented earlier, there are many benefits to be gained. The involvement of a nominated individual from the collaborating establishment as a supervisor to the project appears to reap particular benefits.

References

Phillips, E. (1980) Education for research: the changing constructs of the postgraduate. *International Journal of Man-Machine Studies 13*, 39–48.

Phillips, E. and Pugh, D. (1987) *How to Get a PhD*. Milton Keynes: Open University Press.

Rudd, E. (1990) The early careers of social science graduates and the value of a PhD. *Journal of the Royal Statistical Society 153*, 203–232.

Rudd, E. and Hatch, S. (1968) *Graduate Study and After*. London: Weidenfeld and Nicholson.

Whitehand, J. (1966) The selection of research students. *University Quarterly 21*, 44–48.

Wilkinson, A. (1989) The supervision of higher degrees in education. *Supervision in Education 39*, 45–50.

Wright, J. and Lodwick, R. (1989) The process of the PhD: a study of the first year of doctoral study. *Research Papers in Education 4*, 22–56.

Chapter 9

Doctoral Social Scientists and the Labour Market

Helen Connor[1]

Introduction

During the 1980s higher education has expanded rapidly with the numbers in the applied social sciences, such as business and administrative studies, growing particularly fast. At postgraduate level there has been an expansion in both taught courses and research studies: in 1990 over 8000 students graduated with higher degrees in social science disciplines, an increase of over 25 per cent since 1986. Within this total, only a small proportion, just over 1 in 10, were doctoral students.

Postgraduate training is recognised as having a number of overlapping roles, which include the provision of training in research techniques, contribution to knowledge and the supply of highly qualified and trained people to the labour market (Blum 1986). In respect of the latter, precise manpower planning has been shown to be inappropriate and impractical (Bosworth and Pearson 1992, Izatt and Pearson 1981, Psacharopoulos 1991) when planning future provision of postgraduate training. Public policy bodies (i.e. Research Councils, ABRC, Government) and employers, as well as would-be students, need to be aware of the pattern of postgraduate training, its effectiveness, its linkages with employment and labour market trends if they are to take appropriate decisions about supporting or entering it.

Various concerns have been expressed in the past at government level and among employers and academia about the quality and outcome of social science research training (see, for example, Winfield 1987). Little systematic evidence has existed about the extent and nature of employer demand for doctoral social scientists and on

---

1   The IMS research team who undertook this study comprised Richard Pearson, Ian Seccombe, Geoffrey Pike, Sarah Holly and Helen Connor.

training needs. To help remedy these shortcomings, the ESRC, as part of its initiative on Research Training, commissioned a study at the Institute of Manpower Studies (IMS) which aimed to explore the nature of the demand for doctoral social scientists in the labour market and the flow from doctoral study into employment (Pearson *et al.* 1991)

Definitions and scope

There are no clearly and commonly agreed definitions of the disciplines and activities that make up the social sciences, a situation which is becoming more problematic by the growing number of multidisciplinary activities and the changing nature of postgraduate study itself (e.g. growth in part-time courses). For the purposes of this study some boundaries had to be drawn. Social sciences was defined in broad terms to include doctoral study in: economics, sociology, social psychology, human geography, politics, law, business and related management and financial studies.[2]

Education was excluded from the main focus of the study because the vast majority of their graduates enter the education employment sector and their labour market is quite distinct from other groups.

The emphasis throughout the research study was on the output from full-time doctoral study as this represents the main flow of new skills at this level onto the labour market. Although part-time training is an increasingly popular option, and plays a significant role in research training, many who register for part-time PhDs are already in employment with quite different career concerns than those on full-time study. It was felt to be more appropriate that they should be subject to a separate study rather than be incorporated into this piece of research, which already had a wide scope.

The research aimed to address the central question of what the labour market for doctoral social scientists looks like. In doing so, it provided new, and more comprehensive, information and data about the output of social science graduates and their flow into employment and to other destinations, the strength of demand for PhD/DPhil graduates in key sectors of the economy, and the contribution of research training to the initial employment and early careers of social scientists.

---

2   These categories coincide with the USR subject classification, the main statistical source on students and academic staff data – Group 9 (Social Sciences), Group 10 (Business and Financial Studies) and Group 16 (Multidisciplinary Studies).

The research took place during late 1989 and 1990 and included several key components:

1. A detailed review and analysis of existing information and statistics to map out the terrain and refine the other parts of the study.

2. A survey of social science departments in HEIs and independent research centres (165 in all, a response rate of 65%) to collect data on a subject basis about the student population, demand for research training places, graduate destinations, departmental links with employers and staffing issues.

3. Analysis and statistical modelling of data relating to the academic sector, the major employment destination of doctoral graduates, to explore the likely requirements under various assumptions about retention and staffing levels.

4. A survey of over 850 employers in industry, commerce and the public sector (a 57% response rate) and follow-up interviews with a small sub-sample (21) to seek data on their employment and recruitment of social science PhD/DPhils and their views on the relevance of social science research training.

5. A survey of over 350 PhD/DPhil students (a 50% response rate) who completed their studies between 1985 and 1988, to obtain their experiences and views of entering the labour market, their subsequent training and career progress, and their perceptions of the relevance of doctoral training in their jobs.

One of the key points arising from this, and indeed earlier, research (see for example Clarke and Rees 1988, Connor and Pearson 1990, Izatt and Pearson 1981) is that the labour market for doctoral social scientists is extremely small and fragmented, and inexorably linked with the labour market for first degree and master's level graduates; it also varies between the constituent social science subjects. As such it is wrong to think of doctoral social scientists as forming a distinct group in the labour market. This should be borne in mind when reading this chapter, especially when aggregations of data are used.

The discussion which follows concentrates on some key features of the research findings, namely: the flow of PhD or DPhil social science graduates into employment; their experiences of finding and entering employment; the main employment prospects. Before presenting data on the employment scene it is worthwhile looking briefly at some output figures.

Doctoral output

As mentioned above, only a small proportion of postgraduates qualify at doctoral level. This total was 865 in 1989, 11.3 per cent of higher degree social science graduates. Doctoral output has grown by 10 per cent since 1986, but this is less than the rate of growth for all higher degree (27%) and first degree (17%) graduates in social sciences. Nearly half of the total output of doctoral social scientists are overseas students, and the growth in overseas numbers accounts for most of the growth since 1986.

Figure 9.1: PhD output (universities, home and overseas)

Subject	1986	1989	% Overseas	% higher
Economics	116	122	61	16
Sociology	112	93	28	25
Social Policy/Admin	20	22	34	10
Applied Social Work	1	5	N/A	2
Anthropology	41	44	52	39
Psychology	37	40	15	21
Politics	95	126	50	18
Law	50	71	63	7
Other/Combined	46	66	61	15
Business/Financial Studies (total)	147	157	50	5

Source: USR

As Figure 4.1 shows, the three largest subject groups of doctoral graduates are business and financial studies, politics and economics. Numbers have been rising across all subject groups except sociology. Overseas students have the highest representations in economics, law and 'other/combined' categories.

The proportion of doctoral graduates within the total higher degree output varies markedly by subject: it is highest in geography and anthropology where over 1 in 3 postgraduates are at doctoral level, and lowest in business/financial studies and applied social work (less than 1 in 20). Only 3 per cent of PhD/DPhil social science graduates studied at a polytechnic or college in 1989, compared with 9 per cent of all higher degree graduates.

Employment destinations

First destination statistics

An assessment of the recorded destinations six months after the award of doctorate showed that one third of 1989 graduates were in permanent employment, a third had gone overseas (almost all of whom were overseas students), while the destinations of most of the remainder were unknown. These data, from the survey of First Destinations of Graduates (USR annual), are inadequate on two main grounds: first, they relate to the time of the award not the time of completion of full-time study which may differ by several years; and second they exclude those who fail to receive the PhD. It was for these main reasons that it proved necessary to undertake a survey of social science departments and students (see component 2 above).

Departmental survey

The departmental survey covered almost 400 individual students in 165 departments who completed their full-time studies in 1988/89. It showed that the main employment destination of PhD students in the UK was lecturing or research posts in higher education (30% of the total). Less than 10 per cent entered private industry or commerce and a similar percentage entered the public sector (Figure 9.2). Little change over time was noted by survey respondents, but the very

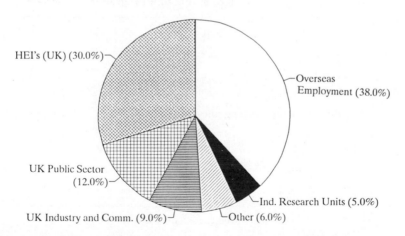

Source: IMS Survey HEIs, 1990

Figure 9.2: Employment destinations of PhDs/DPhils students completing full-time studies in 1988–89

small numbers per department made it difficult for them to general-
ise trends in destination patterns. Where a trend was evident, it was
invariably a shift away from academic employment to the private
sector especially but also to the public sector and overseas.

Student survey

The student survey shed further light on the flow into employment.
It included 354 individuals, 1 in 10 of all home students completing
studies in the period 1985–88. Almost half were aged over 35 years
at the time of the survey, and 35 per cent were women. One in five
were overseas students, a much smaller proportion than in the population as a whole. It should be noted also that because of the way the
survey sample was generated it over-represented both students who
had obtained their doctorates and ESRC funded students compared
to the population as a whole.

Only one in four of the student respondents had not started any
job seeking activities before they had finished their full-time study.
Those who had not been in full-time employment prior to commenc-
ing doctoral studies were most likely to start their job search earlier,
probably attributable to the ever-diminishing resources of students

Figure 9.3: Type of work sought by PhD/DPhil graduates (1985–88)

	%
Teaching/Lecturing	51
Post-doctoral research	49
non-HEI R & D work	25
Admin/general management	7
Financial work	3
Legal work	2
Other types	25
Base N = 354	

Note: Respondents were allowed more than one response

Source: IMS Survey of Graduates, 1990

who have spent lengthy times in higher education. There was little difference between disciplines or types of funding.

Most were looking to work in academia either in post-doctoral study or teaching posts (see Figure 9.3); under a third had been actively considering working in a non-research environment. Doctoral students graduating from the more vocational disciplines were less likely to have sought post-doc research positions than other social science disciplines: for example at the two extremes only 8 per cent of business studies compared with 61 per cent of sociologists had done so. There was little difference by discipline in the percentages seeking teaching posts in higher education.

The major difficulty experienced in their job search was a shortage of suitable vacancies: almost one half felt that this had been a very significant variable in their job search. Next in order of significance was mobility or being restricted in choice of location (20% considered this factor to be very significant). The latter may be a reflection of their age; other research has shown that degree of employment mobility decreases with age affecting in particular those in their late twenties and thirties (see for example Atkinson 1987). Those students who were seeking to work outside academia frequently mentioned being over-qualified, that their experience was too narrowly based and that their research studies were not considered relevant by employers. These problems are not unique to postgraduate students – they are often experienced too by first degree students – but, as shown below in the views of employers, they are of more significance to the more highly qualified, and often more specialised, graduates.

Overall, economics and business graduates reported the least difficulty in finding suitable employment: only 25 per cent of economists and 21 per cent of business studies graduates reported any degree of difficulty; the comparable percentage among sociologists was 50 per cent.

Despite some difficulty, 85 per cent of the students reported that they had found 'suitable employment'. Two out of three remained in the academic sector, with slightly more (37%) taking up lecturing posts than post-doctoral fellowships (30%). Most of the remainder entered other types of work outside the academic sector. As might be expected, doctoral students from certain disciplines were more likely to take up academic work, at least initially more than 70 per cent of psychologists, sociologists and economists did so compared with 36 per cent and 38 per cent of business students and geographers respectively.

Two-thirds of those students who took up academic posts said that their first job was very related to their doctoral study. This was true of only half of that total in industry, commerce and public services.

This is a reflection of the quite different labour markets; non-HE employers generally place much less emphasis upon doctoral qualifications (with the exception of a few very specialist disciplines and jobs). This applies more broadly than the social sciences but the low value put on a PhD by most employers is more prevalent in social science than science and technology generally.

On the whole, few students pointed to any shortcomings in their doctoral training and more advantages were mentioned, such as research experience (over 50% consider this a very significant benefit in carrying out their first job), and required for an academic career (60% considered it very significant benefit in obtaining first job). With regard to the latter, only 31 per cent of university staff in social sciences actually possess a doctorate. Although this proportion is increasing there would appear to be a mis-match between graduates' perceptions of what is a requisite and reality.

Those who had followed a non-academic career were more likely to indicate shortcomings than others, mentioning more often lack of training in personal skills as a significant factor (42% compared with 19%), and irrelevance to the world of work (30% compared with 13%). The non-HE employers, however, had generally received the additional training they thought they needed from their employers (Figure 9.4).

Figure 9.4: First Job - Perceived Shortcomings of doctoral study: Percentage rating each factor as significant

	Academic	Non-Academic
a) Getting job:		
Irrelevance to world of work	13	33
Lack of training in personal skills	19	37
No financial experience	21	23
b) Doing job:		
Irrelevance to world of work	15	27
No financial experience	26	23

Perceptions of the level of relevance of academic study are interesting. Those entering academe are likely to consider it necessary for the furtherance of their career, and so are highly unlikely to consider it irrelevant. Those entering other areas of work, however, see the qualification as unimportant to employers who give it little credence and consequently the graduates are more likely to view it as being unimportant too. Similarly with the development of personal skills – e.g. team working, assertiveness, presentation and communication skills – where those following a non-academic career felt they were at a disadvantage compared with people who had not done a doctorate, but had gained three plus years experience instead. Overall, lack of training in personal skills was seen as the major shortcoming of doctoral study (24% overall took this view).

Employment opportunities outside HE

It is clear from the above that the academic sector remains the major employer of doctoral social scientists. We wished, however, to review the employment opportunities right across the economy and sought to include in the study a wide range of employers in the private and public sectors. This proved to be difficult because of a lack of a reliable and easily accessible sampling frame and employers' low levels of interest in postgraduate training in the social sciences. In many cases there was scepticism about the relevance to them of postgraduate study, which affected their propensity to respond to the questionnaire survey and their grasp of the key issues. This was not unlike the experience of the ESRC Training Board in getting responses to its 'green paper' in 1989, which received a derisory response from the top industrial companies, public sector organisations and management/business consultancies.

Few employers outside academe have a specific demand for doctoral social scientists, and as a consequence few hold detailed information about their employment, in particular by discipline. Out of a total of 630 employers covering all sectors, 56 per cent acknowledged they employed staff with postgraduate qualifications in social science disciplines, but just 25 per cent employed social science doctorates. The key sectors were independent research institutes (67% with any social science PhD graduates) and central government (40%).

An indicator of the small size of the recruitment market is shown by the intake figures. We found that the 120 organisations employing any PhD graduates had recruited between them a total of 256 in the last five years, and only 45 in the last 12 months. Only one in ten had recruited more than five over the five-year period. Smaller employers accounted for a disproportionate share of those recruited; almost half of all PhD graduates recruited in the last five years had joined small/medium sized enterprises (SMEs, with fewer than 250 staff). There has been a slight increase in the overall intake figures over the five-year period: the reasons behind this upward trend included changes in job contents, the availability of better candidates, as well as organisational growth. Overall, there has been a slight shift away from the public sector and business/financial services towards the independent research institutes.

Given the small and widely scattered nature of the demand for social science PhDs it was not surprising to find few employers with a specific recruitment strategy. They were largely an invisible subset of the broader graduate intake. In the few instances that they were specifically sought, mainly for research jobs, employers had used their links with particular HEIs. Despite the small number of vacancies, employers still reported difficulties in attracting the staff they wanted. The most common complaints were: poor quality, inappropriate skills and unrealistic salary expectations.

Personal qualities, in particular motivation, interpersonal skills, maturity, independence and self-reliance, are increasingly being emphasised in graduate recruiters' specifications, and are often given priority over degree subject, class or level of qualification. As one employer said: 'we recruit them because we like them as people... the PhD is merely an added extra.' However, the combination of increased personal skills and maturity gained during the course of their research studies, and enhanced research and analytical skills and greater knowledge in a specific branch of the social sciences, was sometimes seen as helping postgraduates to initially perform better and be more productive. The vast majority of employers however could see no particular advantage or disadvantage to the employment of doctorates. The time spent on a doctorate was viewed as less relevant than an equivalent period of work experience.

The academic labour market

By contrast, a postgraduate qualification, though less often a doctorate, was a normal entry requirement to the academic sector. Overall half the permanent academic staff in the survey of HEI social science departments had a doctorate qualification. (This proportion is higher than reported earlier from the USR statistics because it is based on a different sample in terms of representation of disciplines.) Doctorates were most commonly sought in sociology departments: 50 per cent of departments considered it a prerequisite compared with 28 per cent on average.

Recruitment difficulties were being experienced by half of the departments in the survey. About 4 per cent of the stock of both research and academic posts represented vacant posts, and just over-one third of academic vacancies had been unfilled for more than 6 months. Difficulties were seen to be greater in disciplines where external market demand was strong, e.g. business studies, law, economics. Polytechnic staff were less likely to report recruitment difficulties than universities.

In total there was an estimated 12000 teaching and research staff in social science departments in the higher education sector in 1989, the largest proportion being at universities (c.8000). The university figure grew by 7 per cent between 1985 and 1989, despite an increased annual leaving rate. Virtually all the employment growth in the period was accounted for by the growth in NWUFs (non-wholly university funded students), which made up 23 per cent of the total in 1989. The staff profile was biased towards men in the upper echelons: only 2 per cent of women were at the professorial grade compared with 11 per cent of men.

Future employment prospects

A wide range of factors will influence the demand for graduates and postgraduates over the rest of this decade, not least of which will be the timing and nature of the economic recovery. The current recession (in the early 1990s) is having a depressed effect on recruitment intakes in industry and all levels are down considerably on the late 1980s. It is unlikely that these will recover to anything like previous levels in the near future. The changing financial arrangements within higher education and the rate of expansion of the student population are key factors likely to affect the academic market.

Few employers in our survey were able to forecast future requirements for social science PhD graduates, but then few were expecting to target this group. Only 10 per cent were expecting requirements to increase and 5 per cent expected a decrease, but insufficient data could be obtained to project the level of future demand, even over the next 2–3 years. If an increased requirement does come through, it is more likely to be at the master's than the doctorate level. The main growth sectors are health, financial and business services and independent research centres. However, most projections of future demand for graduates have had to be revised downwards since our survey took place in 1990, because of the impact of the recession on businesses and constraints on public sector budgets. It is likely that we will see little, if any, expansion in demand for social science doctorates over the next few years.

More optimistic expectations came out of higher education where recruitment needs *were* expected to expand during the 1990s mainly as a result of the growth in student numbers over the decade. The existence of high quality data from the USR on stocks and flows of staff affecting the university sector enabled us to model a series of scenarios to project likely recruitment needs in the universities under differing assumptions about staffing levels and wastage rates. (It is impossible to undertake a similar exercise for the non-HE sector, or the non-university sector, because of lack of data.)

The analysis used a projection model within the IMS-WASTAGE software package (since revised and developed into the SUSSEX model). Various runs of the model were made, starting with the most simple case which projected the number of recruits required to maintain the current (1989) level of stocks assuming current levels of wastage and a current age profile, and then building in alternative assumptions about age-related wastage rates and growth rates. For the latter, various scenarios were developed based on assumptions (albeit necessarily rather crude) of student projections and likely changes in staff:student rates. Two scenarios are exemplified below:

(i) If current staffing levels are maintained and current wastage levels prevail (10.3% of stock) then the number of recruits needed to enter the universities would rise from an average of 815 in the early 1990s to 870 by 2005.

(ii) If, on the other hand, the number of posts were to expand to reflect the growth in student numbers but with a slightly falling staff:student ratio, and wastage rates were to increase by 10 per cent, then recruitment needs could rise to a figure of 1200 or more per annum by 2000.

These projections need to be compared with the historical trends of the late 1980s, which show that intakes rose from 776 in 1987 to 1233 in 1989. Under most scenarios it became clear that 1990–99 intakes are unlikely to exceed those prevailing in the late 1980s.

Summary details of these projections are shown in Figure 9.5. It is interesting to note that under the higher growth scenario the social science academic population would get somewhat younger, with the proportion under 35 rising to nearly 25 per cent by 2000.

Figure 9.5: Projected Recruitment to Universities 1990-2000, with variable wastage and high growth assumptions

Target Staff-in-post Year 2000	Wastage Assumption	Staff: Student Ratio	Recruitment			10 Year Average
			1990	1995	2000	
9567	Current	12	979	1057	1157	1064
10716	Current	10.5	1090	1234	1388	1239
10716	High (+10%)	10.5	1144	1300	1465	1304
10716	Low (-10%)	10.5	981	1109	1248	1113
7881	Current	N/A	815	802	826	814

Note: 7881 = staff-in-post 1989 (i.e. maintain current stock, zero growth)

Conclusions

The late 1980s has seen a continuing rise in the number of doctorate graduates in social sciences, though in relation to the total graduate population they represent a very small group. The majority of doctoral graduates seek and obtain teaching or research posts in higher education, in a subject area closely related to their area of research. Less than one-third enter jobs outside the academic sector, generally in a field not directly related to their doctoral study.

The research has highlighted the two quite distinct labour markets for doctoral graduates. On the one hand, the HE sector which takes the lion's share, where considerable emphasis is given to their qualification and their doctoral research work in getting and doing their initial jobs; while on the other, the non-academic market, which is small and very fragemented, and largely invisible. The research has also highlighted significant differences between social science disciplines which need to be given greater emphasis in any future labour market analysis work.

Despite some difficulties, mainly because of a lack of vacancies, the vast majority of recent PhD graduates found what they described as suitable employment. The main benefit of doing a PhD in the social sciences was the development of research techniques and research experience, especially for those aiming for an academic career. Perceived shortcomings of postgraduates' study included the development of personal skills and, for those working in the non-academic sector, overspecialisation and a lack of relevant work experience. To some extent these mirror the problems which many first degree social science graduates face, as employers increasingly put emphasis in recruitment on 'person and potential' rather than degree qualification.

It is clear from this and other research (see Bulmer, McKennel and Schonhardt-Bailey 1992) that there is a danger in over-emphasising the PhD as the only route to research training or a research career, even in academe. Few non-academic employers actively seek social science doctorates and where they are recruited for research posts they are often considered alongside MSc or even first degree graduates. Master's level training is often seen as being of more use to prospective employers. In the academic sector where more emphasis is given to doctoral study in recruitment specifications, rarely is a PhD a necessary requirement for a post.

In the future, there is not expected to be any significant change in demand for doctoral social scientists in the non-academic sector and their employment opportunities will largely reflect the changing demand for first degree graduates in the economy. Demand in the academic labour market is likely to rise if there is a significant increase in academic posts, but this in turn is dependent on the level of HE finance and the rate of expansion of the student base.

References

Association of Graduate Recruiters (AGR) *The AGR Salary and Vacancy Survey*. Bi-annual series of reports by IMS for AGR, Cambridge.

Atkinson, J. (1987) *Relocating Managers and Professional Staff*. IMS Report, No 139. Brighton: Institute of Manpower Studies.

Blum, S. (1986) The development and current dilemmas of postgraduate. *European Journal of Education 21*, No.3.

Bosworth, D. and Pearson, R. (1992) Shortages of professional scientists and engineers. In D. Bosworth *et al. Skill Shortages: Causes and Consequences*. Hants: Avebury.

Bulmer, M., McKennel, A. and Schonhardt-Bailey, C. (1992) *Training in Quantitative Methods for Postgraduate Social Scientists: The Other Side of the Fence*. Paper to Research Training in the Social Sciences Conference, Cambridge, September 1992.

Clarke, J. and Rees, A. (1988) The 1980 graduate cohort study: Where are they now?. *Employment Gazette*, September 1988.

Connor, H. and Pearson, R. (1990) *Manpower Demand for Postgraduate Social Scientists*. Brighton: Institute of Manpower Studies.

Izatt, A. and Pearson, R. (1981) *The Employment of Postgraduate Social Scientists*. Brighton: Institute of Manpower Studies.

Pearson, R., Seccombe, I., Pike, G., Holly, S. and Connor, H. (1991) *Doctoral Social Scientists and the Labour Market*, IMS Report No 217. Brighton: Institute of Manpower Studies.

Psacharopoulos, G. (1991) From manpower planning to labour market analysis. *International Labour Review* Vol.130, No.4.

USR (annually) *First Destination Statistics 1979–1991*. Cheltenham: University Funding Council.

Winfield, G. (1987) *The Social Science PhD*. Swindon: ESRC.

Chapter 10

Training in Quantitative Methods for Postgraduate Social Scientists
The Other Side of the Fence

Martin Bulmer, Aubrey McKennell
and Cheryl Schonhardt-Bailey

The focus in this chapter shifts from an examination of training of postgraduate social science students within higher education, the concern of the majority of the chapters in this book, to look at the issues from the point of view of those in the wider labour market for social researchers, whether as employers or as research workers. Most of the projects in the Research into Training Programme studied aspects of the process of research training before postgraduate students move into employment. The project on *Employers' and Researchers' Experiences of Postgraduate Training in Quantitative Methods* examined the issues with which it was concerned from the other side of the fence, from the standpoint of those who were either employing postgraduate social scientists as research staff, or were working themselves as research staff, having graduated in social science subjects within the last five years.

Its concerns were thus both wider and narrower than some of the other research reported here. It was wider in that it was concerned with people employed in 'social research' posts, rather than just in 'social science research' or as 'social scientists'. The variety of employment sectors for social researchers are discussed more fully below, and extend far beyond teaching and research posts in the academic world. Indeed one of the major issues which this chapter raises is the degree of articulation between training in academic social sciences at postgraduate level and the demands and circumstances of those in social research employment. The fit is by no means a close or comfortable one, and in one or two sectors such as market research we found little evidence of direct connection.

Our research was also narrower, being concerned not with research training in general but with quantitative competence. The central question with which this research was concerned was how well social science training in different subjects equipped its graduates once in the labour market to conduct various types of quantitative research, particularly social survey research. This question remains an important one for British social science. It is part of a wider issue of numeracy, the literature on which (e.g. Crump 1990, Paulos 1989) continues to be a reminder of the broader issues involved. The extent of numeracy among young people who have passed through the English educational system is well below the general level of literacy, a significant proportion falling short of an adequate standard of numerical understanding on leaving education. Premature specialisation within the school system, after taking GCSE at the age of 16, is one cause of this. In England and Wales, unlike Scotland, pupils pursuing academic studies are expected at the age of 16 to narrow down their subject choice to two, three or four subjects studied in depth at 'A' level. For a majority of students this means giving up the further study of mathematics or statistics, and for many a choice between science subjects which tend to be more quantitative, and humanities and social science subjects which are largely non-quantitative.[1]

The problem of quantitative competence

The split between more quantitative and less quantitative subjects persists at university within the undergraduate curriculum. Although the pattern is more differentiated than in the last two years at school there remains a broad division between subjects which require mastery of at least some parts of post-GCSE mathematics or statistics, and sometimes an advanced level of understanding, and those where treatment of quantitative methods is either nominal or nonexistent. In the former category are many areas of science, technology and engineering, as well as many departments of psychology,

---

1   This is true of some social science 'A' levels. Sociology, economics and geography are all popular 'A' level subjects which may lead on to the study of those subjects and other social sciences at university. None of them, however, are heavily quantitative, and the student studying them, to the extent that they require quantitative competence, will find that acquired at GCSE sufficient. There is little progression beyond that level. This is in marked contrast to the student who studies mathematics, statistics or physics at 'A' level, or the undergraduate who studies econometrics or quantitative geography, where for some courses at British universities 'A' level mathematics or statistics may be an entry requirement.

economics and in some cases geography; in the later category most
of the humanities and (in many though not all departments) social
sciences such as political science, sociology and social policy.

This state of affairs, so far as it affects the social sciences, has been
commented upon by a number of reviews. The Social Research
Association's report on *The State of Training in Social Research* (1985)
identified nineteen areas in which there were omissions in the research training coverage provided at undergraduate or postgraduate
level, including a number where the absence of training was very
marked, including computing packages, multivariate statistics, coding, content analysis, cross tabulation, attitude scaling and project
management. Factor analysis of data from a membership survey of
the Social Research Association revealed that disciplines varied in
their coverage of clusters of areas, business management being the
only area to score high on data collection issues, economics, statistics
and psychology scoring low. In data analysis, geography, statistics
and business management scored high, compared with sociology
and political science which scored low to medium on this factor and
on data collection (SRA 1985 pp.12–13).

Two years later, the international group on *Horizons and Opportunities for the Social Sciences*, reviewing the future of the social sciences
over the next ten years, chaired by Professor Griffith Edwards, commented sharply on failings in quantitative competence in some fields
of British social science:

> In the interviews conducted as background to this report a sense
> of weariness emerged as yet another informant said that British
> social science is facing a numeracy problem... (T)here is a very
> real worry that in some subjects (sociology and political science
> for example) researchers are not as numerate as their colleagues
> overseas and the gap is widening. This must be of deep concern
> given the growing importance of research areas at the meeting
> points of disciplines... (A)t worst some social scientists appear to
> show not only indifference but disdain for statistical training.
> (Horizons 1987 p.7)

Postgraduate training policy by the Economic and Social Research
Council from the late 1980s took on board the need to take action. The
Winfield Report (1987) commented trenchantly on inadequacies of
training in this area, and the Training Guidelines promulgated by the
ESRC Training Board in 1991, coming into effect for holders of ESRC
studentships in October 1992, put considerable emphasis upon reme-
dying past omissions.

Public comment on the problems of inadequate numeracy among
British graduates continues. To give but two examples, at a general

level, the Association of Graduate Recruiters has commented on shortcomings in numeracy and problem solving skills found among recent graduates entering the labour market (*The Guardian* July 9, 1991). Specifically in relation to social science postgraduates, the flagship ESRC interdisciplinary research centre on Micro-Social Change at the University of Essex found at the outset a lack of suitable applicants for their new establishment. Professor A.P.M. Coxon and Mr D. Rose, Director and Deputy Director, wrote to the *Times Higher Education Supplement* in the autumn of 1989 to comment on the difficulty of recruiting well qualified quantitative researchers to the staff who would conduct the British Household Panel Study.

The four studies

With this starting point, our project set out in 1989 to 1991 to investigate how the problem was perceived, not primarily within higher education itself, but by those in the labour market where some of the products of postgraduate social science worked upon empirical social research. Our aim was to investigate the issues by means of surveys of research managers on the one hand, and of recently recruited social researchers on the other, complemented by some data from those concerned with the academic training of quantitative researchers. The main effort was devoted to the first two of these, the third stage being more limited by comparison. Before embarking upon the surveys of managers and recent recruits we found it necessary to conduct a prior piece of research, to map the extent and distribution of social research employment in the UK. The study as a whole thus had four components. The present chapter reports on the first and third, the mapping of British social research and the survey of recent recruits.

In addition, we conducted a telephone survey of 241 research managers drawn from the various sectors of research identified in the mapping exercise, and sent a mail questionnaire to 58 academic trainers whom we identified as being particularly responsible either for specialist master's courses in research methods or research training of doctoral social science students. This part of the research is not reported here, and the data are currently being analysed.[2]

---

2   The survey of managers, conducted by the British Market Research Bureau, was based on a questionnaire containing 72 items, administered by telephone interviewers using a computer-aided telephone interviewing system. 419 addresses were issued, with the aim of achieving 240 interviews. There were 14 refusals, 27 respondents had ex-directory numbers, and 137 were not contactable or unavailable. The number of completed interviews,

Employment in social research in Britain

Before studying the social research labour market, it was necessary to define it. Since 'social science' and 'social research' are not synonymous with one another, this was in part a definitional problem and in part an empirical question. The definitional problem was apparent from the difference between social researchers and the conventional division of academic knowledge and personnel into disciplines and learned societies, for example sociologists in the British Sociological Association, political scientists in the Political Studies Association, economists in the Royal Economic Society, and so on. Most British universities are organised into departmental units whose identity derives from the academic disciplines which they profess. Many contain research staff within them, but their identity is defined in terms of the academic disciplines which they teach.

The activity of empirical 'social research' is organised differently, and predominantly outside academia. The membership of the Social Research Association represents the range and variety of locations for such research. In 1992, for example, one-fifth of its members worked in market research, one in six in central government, one in ten in each of independent institutes and in local government, one in five in educational institutions and one in six elsewhere (SRA 1992). The SRA membership list did not of itself provide an adequate sampling frame for our study, since its coverage of the sectors in which social researchers work was uneven and limited, and even in major central government units and independent institutes it was clear only a small proportion of staff belonged to the association. We therefore concluded that we should construct our own sampling frame by mapping the different sectors of social research, with particular reference

---

with substitution allowed, was 241. The typical interview lasted 20–25 minutes. Some questions used were the same in the managers' and the recruits' surveys, and this will permit more detailed comparisons between the two groups. The survey of academic trainers, which also used some of the same questions, was the least satisfactory of the three exercises. Its scale had to be curtailed due to both time pressures, timing (which coincided with the ESRC recognition exercise for research student training in 1991) and to uncertainty as to how many respondents would be sufficiently centrally concerned with training and interested to respond to the questionnaire during the summer vacation. In the event we received 27 responses, a response rate of just under 50 per cent. Indirectly, the response rate and several of the comments we received support the interpretation we offer of the lack of fit between academic social science and the profession of social research, particularly outside the academic world.

to quantitative social research. We therefore proceeded to attempt to establish how many people doing quantitative social research there were in different areas of employment.

Mapping the research sector: the size and shape of the labour market for quantitative social science research

Research method

No comprehensive listing existed of social research organisations and one needed to be created from widely scattered sources. In order to draw samples of managers at the second stage and of recently recruited researchers at the third stage, it was necessary to establish a sampling frame of organisations employing relevant social research staff. Establishing the frame involved four sub-stages: (i) constructing a database, (ii) sampling from this base, (iii) carrying out a postal survey to identify organisations employing relevant staff (that is social scientists engaged in quantitative social research) and (iv) derivation of weights for population projections.

The labour market for social scientists was stratified by types of potential employers, and a comprehensive listing of organisations made within each stratum. We embarked on a search operation to identify, for each stratum, as many relevant sources of information as we could from the Market Research Society whose Directory contains a listing of all member firms with numbers of research executives, to higher education where the *Commonwealth Universities Yearbook* is inconsistent in its treatment of research, in the main leaving out a large proportion of research staff not on permanent contracts, and omitting many major research centres in the social sciences. In some sectors, such as local authority research, we had to undertake our own sample survey to estimate numbers employed. Various directories and source books were used as shown in the Appendix. Table 10.1 shows the 18 separate employment strata and sub-strata for which we made listings.

The principal exercise once the organisation in different strata had been identified involved a postal questionnaire to employees of social research staff in twelve different sectors, to obtain estimates of the numbers of staff in each employed on work involving quantitative social research. Some of the sectors, such as local government, were divided into sub-sectors. 1538 one-page questionnaires were issued, and 1025 replies received. All of these were sent out ourselves, with the exception of the survey of academic social research staff, which was carried out as an adjunct to a survey being carried out by the Institute of Manpower Studies as part of their study of *Doctoral*

**Table 10.1: Showing by employment stratum, the number
of organisations sampled, the number of graduate
staff doing quantitative social research, the weights
applied and labour market projections**

	No. of sampled organis- ations (weighted)	No. of staff in sampled organis- ations	Weight Applied	Total No. of staff (weighted)	Total recruited in last five years
Central government	16	555	1.31	727	249
Quango	44	192	1.14	219	96
Nationalised industry	35	25	1.03	26 3	
Probation research	53	61	1.98	121	54
Local government:					
Miscellaneous	7	44	1.98	87	50
Housing	90	91	1.98	180	121
Social services	76	149	1.98	295	191
Planning	111	315	1.98	623	325
Chief Executive's					
Department	77	114	1.98	226	129
Higher education					
IMS Sample	150	472	3.64	1720	@
Research centres	48	340	1.19	404	167
Health research					
Units	56	373	1.50	560	125
Market research	41	466	5.71	2660	828
PLC	43	189	2.00	378	170
Independent institutes	31	178	2.45	436	66
Voluntary society	58	78	1.73	135	85
Health authority	64	110	1.50	165	92
Management					
Consultancy	25	119	1.40	167	32
Total	**1025**			**9129**	

@ = not available

Students in the Labour Market (Pearson *et al.* 1991). The responses to the questionnaire gave certain basic information about the numbers and characteristics of social research staff employed and gave us a count of the number of social scientists employed in quantitative research by the organisations included in our postal sample.

Table 10.1 shows the weights we applied in order to gross up the sample counts. The weights vary between strata according to the sampling method employed. For the seven strata where there was an attempt at a census of organisations the weight needed only to make an allowance for the non-response. For market research, the five local government strata, voluntary societies and PLCs, where we employed surrogate size measures in the sampling, the weight was the ratio of the count on the surrogate size measures in the population to the count in the sample. Further details of the technical aspects of the weighting are available from the principal investigators.

Findings

The main objective of the work, the results of which are presented in Tables 10.2 and 10.3, was to construct a frame which would allow the representative sampling of individual research managers and their recently recruited social research staff doing quantitative social research, for phases two and three of the study. A valuable and unexpected by-product of this work was the picture obtained of the size and shape of the labour market for social researchers in Britain. Here we comment only on some leading features. Full information of this kind has not been previously available, apart from one 'guesstimate' produced in the late 1980s and not published. That estimate was produced by the Social Research Association Post Employment Study Group. It considered that 'at least 5000 and possibly as many as 20000 people (are) engaged in social research in its widest sense as their primary task'.

We estimate that the numbers of graduates employed on quantitative social research in the United Kingdom is of the order of 9000. Seventy per cent of them are outside higher education. Of these social researchers, about 40 per cent have a higher degree. (At this stage of the enquiry we did not distinguish between master's and PhD). These figures are approximations, given the variable responses we received from different sectors to our initial questionnaire, shown above. Our data refer to social research staff doing quantitative work, and hence would produce a lower figure than the total for all social researchers. Our more precise estimate is within the range given by the SRA study group.

Our data give some impression of the shape of professional social research in Britain in 1990, at the time the first phase was carried out. The findings emphasise the extent to which academic social science and professional social research are distinct areas of activity, though there are points of overlap. Three sectors contain three-quarters of quantitative social researchers. The two main employment sectors are market research and higher education, both with 29 per cent of the labour market. Although equal in size, these two major sectors differ markedly in the extent to which they employ graduates with a higher degree. Forty-six per cent of graduates with a higher degree doing quantitative social research are to be found in the higher education sector, compared with only 6 per cent in market research. Almost all entrants to market research possess only a first degree, and their training in research is mainly acquired on the job and on in-house training courses after entering what is known in the trade as the 'market research industry'.

The data for higher education include only research staff: teaching staff are excluded. The location of these research staff is variable. Some work in large and medium size dedicated research centres, financed by organisations such as the Economic and Social Research Council, the Medical Research Council, the Department of Health and the Department of Social Security. Others work on research projects funded by grants to individual members of the academic teaching staff, and are located in teaching departments (though not infrequently housed away from the centre of the department). A considerable number of academic research staff are dispersed in pockets of one, two or three staff per department working on such individual projects. Whatever their location, few research staff have the permanent tenured employment still enjoyed by many university lecturers, although many are pursuing long-term research careers via a series of appointments.

Local government is the next sizeable sector, comprising 17 per cent of all graduates, and the same percentage of graduates with a higher degree. Within local government, researchers are particularly concentrated in departments of housing, planning and social services, and in chief executives' and central planning units. There are very few researchers employed in local authority education departments. Central government, independent institutes and public limited companies are much smaller in size at, respectively 8, 5 and 4 per cent. Three out of four graduates working in independent institutes have a higher degree, about the same concentration in relative terms as in higher education. Central government researchers are typically located in research divisions or research groups such as the Home Office Research and Planning Units. Independent institutes, such as the Policy Studies Institute or Social and Community Planning Research, are organisations dedicated wholly to different kinds of social research.

Health authorities, quangos, voluntary societies (charities) and 'other' (consisting of nationalised industries and management consultants) form even smaller sectors of the labour market, at around 2 per cent each. Health is a significant employment sector for social research when health authorities and academic health research centres are grouped together. Research in the voluntary sector is concentrated in those charities who employ research staff. Management consultancy is a small sector but one which is growing in significance.

Further information about the scale and extent of British social research is to be found in the articles and individual entries in the *Directory of Social Research Organisations in the UK, 1993* (Sykes, Bulmer and Schwerzel 1993)

Table 10.2: Showing, for graduates doing quantitative social research, the numbers with first degrees and postgraduate degrees, analysed by employment strata

	Graduates with:		All
	First Degree Only	Higher Degree	Graduates
Employment Stratum	%	%	%
Market research	46	6	29
Higher education	15	46	29
Local government	18	17	17
Central government	6	9	8
Independent institute	3	9	5
Public limited company	6	3	4
Health authority	2	3	2
Quango	2	3	2
Voluntary society	1	2	2
Other	1	2	2
Total	**100**	**100**	**100**
Base for %	5476	3653	9129

Note: Weighted data giving population estimates

The data were also analysed in terms of the subject groupings shown in Table 10.3. Psychology, economics and statistics cover between them 33 per cent of the labour market, followed closely by the subject group geography, political science and sociology at 29 per cent. The proportion of graduates with higher degrees recruited from these two subject groups were roughly in proportion to the size of the subject group sector in the labour market. The same is true for the residual 'Other social sciences' category which has for example 13 per cent of the total labour market and 15 per cent of the graduates with a higher degree. (This large residual category contained a varied range of subjects out of which none predominated: e.g. planning, land management, demography, criminology, operational research, health (including nursing, epidemiology), linguistics, speech therapy, law, journalism, information science, marketing, cultural studies, Afro-Caribbean studies, development studies, architecture, etc.). Natural science and technology accounted for 8 per cent of the labour market and about the same proportion of graduates with higher degrees.

Table 10.3: Showing, for graduates doing quantitative social research, the numbers with first degrees and postgraduate degrees, analysed by subject studied. Weighted data giving population estimates

	Graduates with:		
	First Degree Only	*Higher Degree*	*All Graduates*
Subject Of Degree	%	%	%
Psychology, economics or statistics	31	37	33
Geography, political science, sociology	27	33	29
Other social sciences	11	15	13
Management or Business Studies	7	2	5
Natural science or technology	8	9	8
Arts and humanities	16	4	11
Total	**100**	**100**	**100**
Base for %	5474	3453	8120

The Views of recently recruited social researchers

Research method

In order to pursue our aim of gaining a perspective upon postgraduate education from those who had experienced it as students and moved out into the labour market, we set out to question a representative sample of recently recruited social research staff. Employers of social research staff were identified at the first stage of the research, discussed above, in replies received listing the number of staff employed with particular types of qualification. The 241 research managers sampled at the second stage, not discussed in this paper, were asked to provide the names of up to three of their research staff recruited within the last five years, and these names provided the basis of the sample drawn. (In two or three sectors, supplementary names were obtained by a follow-up questionnaire to boost numbers.) Between March and May 1991, an eight-page questionnaire with 17 questions was sent to 540 recent recruits to social research posts involving qualitative research. ('Recent' was defined as recruited within the last five years). 422 were returned after two reminders, a response rate of 78 per cent.

Questionnaire respondents somewhat over-represented those working in local government and quangos, and under-represented those working in market research, central government and PLCs. To compensate for this, the results which follow are weighted for the distribution of the sample between sectors. The selected results which follow give some of the main findings; analysis is still in progress.

Findings

Social researchers are more likely to be women than men. Of the sample of 422, 60 per cent were women and 40 per cent were men, not distributed equally between the sectors. Throughout this analysis we pay some attention to the variation between research sectors in which people were employed, since there are some marked variations. There were fewest women, just over half, in health authorities and higher education, and the highest proportion of women, over three-quarters of the sample, in market research and independent institutes.

All but two of the respondents had a first degree. 172 or 40.7 per cent of respondents had a master's degree but the proportion varied between sectors, ranging from nearly three-quarters in the voluntary sector to a quarter in local government. One in five, or 20.9 per cent, of respondents, whether or not they had a master's degree, had a doctorate (Table 10.4). This ranged from nearly half of those working in research jobs in higher education to less than one in twenty in market research and local government research. The proportions are shown in Table 10.5.

Table 10.4: Educational qualifications of a sample of recent recruits to social research posts in Britain, 1992

	Does not have a doctoral degree		*Has a doctoral degree*	
Does not have a master's degree	195		54	
		46%		13%
Has a master's	138		34	
		33%		8%
Total	333		88	
		79%		21%

Table 10.5: Proportions of respondents in different sectors possessing a doctorate

Higher education	45%
Independent institutes	33%
Health authority	25%
Quangos	23%
All researchers	20%
Central government	17%
Voluntary sector	9%
Market research	4%
Local government	4%

Possessing a PhD thus appeared to be a more significant qualification (although a minority one) in higher education and independent institutes, less important in health authorities, quangos and central government, and of slight importance in the voluntary sector, market research and local government.

Eighteen per cent of respondents were currently studying part-time for a degree or diploma, ranging from nearly a third in higher education, and a quarter in local government, health authorities and central government to 7 per cent in market research and less than one in twenty in independent institutes. There appeared to be an inverse relationship in some sectors between involvement in part-time study and the availability of training through the employer.

According to respondents, their organisations varied according to whether they had any sort of budget set aside to meet training requirements. All those in central government and most of those in local government and health authorities had a training budget available, but only two-thirds in market research, half in independent institutes and 40 per cent in higher education (the lowest). The low provision for training in higher education is particularly striking, though studying for a higher degree may to some extent be regarded as an alternative.

We had hypothesised at the outset that the perceived relevance of postgraduate work in general and of the PhD in particular would depend upon the content of what had been studied, and how adequate a research training was provided. The differences observed between sectors may be explained partly by the perceived relevance of postgraduate work, and such an explanation accounts for variations between the extremes. In higher education, a PhD is naturally prised as the highest earned academic qualification, in market research any postgraduate qualification appears to be unusual, and not regarded as a necessary entry qualification by employers. The comparatively low proportion of PhDs overall, one in five, a figure even so inflated by the higher proportion among academic researchers, cast doubt *prima facie* about how relevant the PhD was perceived to be as a research training.

One set of questions we asked was concerned with the amount of time social science postgraduates had devoted to research training. The responses relate to the second half of the 1980s. Of the 172 respondents with a master's degree, 111 or 65 per cent had spent time on training in quantitative research as part of their degree. Of these, 17 (15%) had spent all their time, 17 (15%) had spent between a quarter and half their time, and 64 (62%) had spent one-quarter or less of their time.

Of the 88 respondents who had a doctorate, just over half (46) had done work as part of their PhD which involved special training in research methods. (Just under half had not.) Of the 46 with training, 6 (12%) had spent all their time on training activities, 4 (8%) half their time, 7 (14%) between 11 per cent and 25 per cent of their time, and 29 (58%) 10 per cent or less of their time on research training.

Respondents were asked: Looking back on the training in methods of empirical social research which you received when studying at university or polytechnic, how useful did you find it for carrying out your present job? They were asked to rate their reply on a five point scale from 5 = essential to 1 = no use.

The proportions rating such training essential were generally low, varying from over one third in independent institutes to one in twenty five in market research (Table 10.6).

Table 10.6: Proportion of respondents rating university or polytechnic training in methods of empirical social research essential for their present job

Independent institutes	36%
Health authorities	27%
Higher education	22%
Central government	18%
Voluntary organisations	10%
Local government	10%
Market research	4%

The variation was less marked when the mean scores were taken into account.

Table 10.7: Respondents' mean and median scores derived from ratings of the importance of various components of quantitative research training (5 = essential, 1 = not important)

Item	Mean	Median
Simple statistical techniques	4.2	5
Survey analysis	4.2	5
Questionnaire design	4.1	5
Special survey packages e.g. SPSS	3.4	4
Sampling theory	3.3	4
Advanced statistical techniques (e.g. multiple regression, statistical modelling)	2.7	3
Project management	4.0	5
Word processing skills	3.7	4
Database/spread sheet skills	3.4	4

Respondents were then asked to rate the importance of nine items, six relating to quantitative analysis and three to other skills useful in research posts. The mean and median scores on a five point scale are shown in Table 10.7. The higher the mean or the median, the more importantly it was rated.

Table 10.8: Respondents' mean scores by employment sector, derived from ratings of the importance of various components of quantitative research training (5 = essential, 1 = not important)

	Market research	Higher Educn	Local Govt	Central Govt	Ind Inst
Simple statistical techniques	4.3	4.2	3.9	4.6	4.3
Survey analysis	4.6	4.0	4.1	4.3	4.6
Questionnaire design	4.6	4.0	3.6	4.5	4.3
Special survey packages e.g. SPSS	2.3	3.9	3.6	4.5	3.9
Sampling theory	3.9	3.2	3.0	3.8	3.3
Advanced statistical techniques (e.g. multiple regression statistical modelling)	2.6	2.9	2.1	3.0	3.1
Project management	4.2	3.7	3.5	4.6	4.1
Word processing skills	3.0	4.2	3.6	4.7	3.9
Database/spread sheet skills	2.7	3.3	4.0	3.6	3.1
N	112	124	75	35	22

These scores were then calculated for the five main strata, where significant differences emerged, as shown in Table 10.8.

A question was included asking whether the respondent *did* receive training in any of these areas as an undergraduate or postgraduate, shown in Table 10.9.

A further question made an attempt to gauge the importance of the possession of skills in quantitative methods compared with other qualities sought in applicants for research posts. Other evidence suggested that employers in seeking to fill posts do not rate possession of quantitative skills very highly in comparison with other qualities. In interpreting the results, it should be borne in mind that the question relates to staff working on quantitative social research, not to the general labour market. This yielded the pattern shown in

Table 10.9: Proportions of a sample of recent recruits to social research posts who did receive training in different social research skills as an undergraduate or postgraduate

Sector	All	Market Resch	Higher Educn	Local Govt	Central Govt	Indep Inst
Simple stats	65	84	80	86	100	85
Quest. design	54	36	51	67	83	63
Survey analysis	53	37	50	68	78	56
Statistical package	42	35	47	47	74	44
Sampling theory	68	65	67	70	78	82
Advanced stats	63	60	58	58	91	51
Sample	**423**	**112**	**124**	**75**	**35**	**22**

Table 10.10: Ranking of a series of qualities necessary for doing the job of the respondent (first means most important, sixth means least important, = indicates a tie)

Sector	All	Market Resch	Higher Educn	Local Govt	Central Govt	Indep Inst
Good intellectual capacity	second	third=	first=	second=	second	second
Persuasiveness in argument	sixth	sixth	fifth	fifth	fifth	sixth
Ability to write clearly and intelligibly	first	second	first=	first	first	first
Personable and easy to get on with	fifth	third=	fourth	sixth	sixth	fourth
effective in oral communication	third	first	third	second=	third	third
Competence in handling numbers	fourth	third=	sixth	fourth	fourth	fourth

Table 10.10. (Rather than showing raw mean scores on a five-point scale, the table shows the priority accorded among different qualities.)

Competence in handling numbers did not therefore rate very highly compared with other qualities sought in applicants for social research posts. It ranked lowest out of six qualities sought in researchers in higher education, fourth out of six in three other sectors, and third equal in market research. This provides a cautionary reminder that possession of relatively technical skills is not necessarily the prime consideration in recruitment to job positions. The low ranking of quantitative competence among recruits to academic research positions is particularly striking.

Conclusions

The results presented in the second half of this chapter relate to research staff recruited between 1985 and 1990. They were therefore trained as postgraduates in social science in a period before the ESRC had promulgated its Training Guidelines, although one in which from 1987 the first effects of the sanctions policy for completion rates had begun to be felt. The situation in the present may be changing somewhat, as more formal courses are instituted, and a higher level of training is expected of beginning research students. It is less likely that a repeat of this study in the mid-1990s would find as we did that half of those with a PhD working in research posts had no special training in research methods during their doctorate.

Nevertheless, our findings indicate a degree of lack of fit between the PhD (and other social science postgraduate work) and the labour market demands of non-academic social research employment. The content of this training does not adequately cover the kinds of specific research for some of these skills, shown in Tables 10.7, 10.8 and 10.9, and the provision of training among our sample of recent recruits for some of these skills, particularly those of a more practical kind, fell well short of what respondents thought that they needed. We found no evidence whatsoever that respondents thought that they had been overtrained in any particular skill, and a good deal of evidence that they were undertrained. Table 10.6 taken together with Table 10.5 suggests that the relevance of the PhD for a career as a professional social researcher is relatively weakly established.

Evidence from research managers, currently being analysed, was equivocal about the value of a PhD, some recognising its usefulness, some being relatively neutral, others dismissing it in scornful terms as an irrelevance. The latter were in a fairly small minority, but the strength of their feeling, based upon encounters with social science PhDs, was noticeable. On the part of academics, there would be those who would argue that it is not the primary purpose of the PhD to prepare students for non-academic work, and the pursuit of scholarship within a learned discipline is its prime purpose. The standards of evidence and methodological rigour existing within the discipline would determine what training is appropriate. The possibility exists that the sort of criteria utilised by employers in recruiting to social research employment are so different from those of academic supervisors of PhD students, preparing their charges as putative academics, that the two are operating with substantially different criteria. The evidence in Table 10.10 does not entirely support this view, although it serves as a reminder that the possession of specific skills may not be the principal consideration in appointment decisions.

The models of research in operation in sectors of non-academic research employment, for example in market research or in local government, may be substantially different from those operating for the academic PhD. For example, the relatively low importance attached in market research to computing skills (Table 10.8) seems to be accounted for by the employment in many firms of specialist computing staff. Research executives are not expected to do their own computing. Such a division of labour within a large research organisation – there are similarly specialist branches concerned with interviewing and with sampling – is a different pattern from the typical lone PhD project or the small academic project with one or two researchers, which often provides the model for academic training.

The promulgation of the ESRC Training Guidelines, and their adoption from 1992 in most of the major centres of PhD study in the UK, shows a degree of innovation on the part of the social science community, and a wish to enhance the effectiveness of the PhD as a form of research training. The increasing penetration of some social science PhDs into non-academic research employment will also in time increase awareness of the value of the PhD for the professional social researcher. (The case for the value of a master's degree is already better established, market research excepted). Social scientists themselves will have a role to play in educating employers about the value of doctoral work as a preparation for research, and for giving PhD students the opportunities for self-development which will stand them in good stead when entering the labour market. There are prospects that the disjunction between the discipline-based PhD and the sector based professional social researcher will diminish, but active efforts will be needed by both sides to narrow what at present seems an uncomfortably wide gap, not least in relation to training in quantitative research methods.

Appendix: Sources of information in the construction of the sampling frame for mapping the size and shape of the labour market for social researchers

Central government Sources: (1) *Directory of Social Science Research Officers in Government, 1989,* and (2) Social Research Association (SRA) directory. All names from both directories were entered.

Quangos Sources: (1) *The 1989 Civil Service Year Book* (London: HMSO), (2) SRA directory, and (3) *The Training Board Research Forum* list.

Nationalised industries Sources: (1) Phone contact to each nationalised industry (as given in *Vacher's Parliamentary Companion,* No.1055, Aug 1989) to identify the relevant person to whom we could send the questionnaire, (2) listings from SRA (88/89) directory, (3) *1989 Longman Directory of Local Authorities,* for regional water authorities in England, Scotland and Wales, and (4) a list of departments that might employ social science research graduates, from Barry Grant, Operational Research Assistant Manager, British Rail. Selection criteria: all nationalised industries sampled.

Probation officers Source: National Probation Research Information Exchange membership list.

Local government Sources: (1) SRA (88/89) directory, (2) *Longman Directory* for regional housing authorities, (3) *Municipal Year Book 1989* and (4) *INLOGOV Register of Local Government Research 1989,* using population figures for each district. Selected sample of 141 by PPS. We then sent 141 questionnaires (*each*) to housing departments, social services departments, planning departments and chief executive departments.

Higher education – IMS Source: Institute of Manpower Studies survey of one in two universities and polytechnics that had applied to the ESRC for grants. Sent 273 questionnaires, 150 returned.

Higher education research centre Sources: (1) *Current Research in Britain,* Social Sciences Volume, 4th edition and (2) SRA (88/89) directory. The research team went through the list of 520 and determined which of these were research centres.

Higher education health research unit: See below under Health authority.

Market research Sources: (1) *Market Research Year Book* and (2) SRA (88/89) directory. Selection criteria: Selected by probability proportionate to size, using number of executives to indicate size.

Other PLC Sources: (1) *Times 1000 Index* and (2) SRA (88/89) directory. Took all the top 50 firms (in terms of yearly sales) from the Index, and added selected ones chosen by research team from the 51 to 100 category. All in SRA directory were included.

Independent Institutes Sources: (1) SRA (88/89) directory and (2) Association of Social Research Organisations (ASRO) membership list – 1989, as provided by ASRO.

Voluntary societies (Charities) Sources: (1) *Directory of National Voluntary Organisations*, (2) *Charity Trends, 11th Edition (1987)* (A Charities Aid Foundation publication, edited by Judith McQuillan), and (3) SRA (88/89) directory. Took top 50 charities in *Charity Trends'* ranking of top 400 fund-raising charities (sized according to voluntary income), and all charities listed in SRA handbook.

Health authorities and HE Health Research Units Sources: (1) *Society for Social Medicine Membership Directory 1990*, (2) *Medical Sociology in Britain Register* (3) *Longman Directory of Local Authorities* and (4) the *Medical Research Council Listing of Research in the United Kingdom*. Took all research centres listed in *Medical Sociology in Britain* (source 2), took those suggested by K. Dunnell of OPCS from the *Society for Social Medicine Membership Directory* (source 1), took all the regional health authorities listed in the Longman Directory (source 3), took those indicated by the research team from the MRC listing (source 4).

Management Consultancies Source: *Management Consultants Association Directory of Member Firms and Their Services to Clients 1989/90*.

Local government was divided into five strata and higher education into three, for the purposes of listing and sampling. There are interesting and possibly important differences between these sub-strata that would repay further analysis. In order to simplify the work for the present report, however, we have aggregated these sub-strata data at the analysis stage and considered local government and higher education overall.

References

Crump, T. (1990) *The Anthropolgy of Numbers*. Cambridge: Cambridge University Press.

ESRC Training Board (1991) *Research Training Guidelines*. Swindon: Economic and Social Research Council.

The Guardian (July 9th 1991) Employers find graduates ill-equipped for tough jobs market. Story by J Utton Mottle, Education Correspondent.

Horizons (1987) *Horizons ands Opportunities in the Social Sciences.* Report of a working party chaired by Professor Griffith Edwards London: ESRC.

Paulos, J.A. (1989) *Innumeracy: Mathematical Illiteracy and its Consequences.* New York: Viking.

Pearson, R., Seccombe, I., Pike, G., Holly, S. and Connor, H. (1991) *Doctoral Social Scientists in the Labour Market.* IMS Report No.217. Brighton: Institute of Manpower Studies.

SRA (1985) *The State of Training in Social Research: Report of an SRA Subcommittee.* London: Social Research Association.

SRA (1992) *Social Research Association Directory of Members.* London: Social Research Association, 116 Turney Road, London SE21 7JJ.

Sykes, W., Bulmer, M. and Schwerzel, M. (eds) (1993) *Directory of Social Research Organisations in the UK.* London: Mansell.

Winfield Report (1987) *The Social Science PhD: The ESRC Inquiry into Submission Rates.* London: ESRC.

Notes on Contributors

Sandra Acker is a Professor at the Ontario Institute for Studies in Education. She was previously a Lecturer in the School of Education, University of Bristol. She has published on the subject of women and education in journals including the *British Journal of Sociology of Education* and *Sociological Review* and has contributed chapters to a number of collections. She has co-edited the *World Yearbook of Education 1984: Women and Education* (1984) and *Is Higher Education Fair to Women?* (1984). She has also conducted research on teachers' work and culture in primary schools.

Paul Atkinson is Professor of Sociology and Head of the School of Social and Administrative Studies at the University of Wales, Cardiff. His main publications are: *The Clinical Experience, Ethnography: Principles in Practice* (with Martin Hammersley), *Language Structure and Reproduction, The Ethnographic Imagination* and *Understanding Ethnographic Texts.* His main research areas are the sociology of medical knowledge, education and professional socialisation and the development of ethnographic research methods.

Edith Black is a Research Associate on the ESRC funded research project 'Students, Supervisors and the Social Science Research Training Process'. She previously taught English in secondary schools and colleges of further education. She is now a contract researcher in the School of Education at the University of Bristol where she took her MEd in 1984. She recently completed her doctoral thesis which is an ethnographic study of secretarial training in a college of further education.

Martin Bulmer is Professor of Sociology in the Department of Sociology and Social Policy at the University of Southampton. From 1989 to 1992 he was research co-ordinator of the ESRC Training Board Research Into Training Programme, whose research teams are the contributors to this book. Previously, he taught at the London School of Economics and the University of Durham, and worked briefly as a statistician in central government. His recent books include: *The Social Basis of Community Care* (1987), *The Social Survey in Historical Perspective 1880–1940* (co-editor, 1992) and *The Directory of Social Research Organisations in the UK* (co-editor, 1993). He is currently editor of the journal *Ethnic and Racial Studies*.

Robert Burgess is Director of CEDAR (Centre for Educational Development, Appraisal and Research) and Professor of Sociology at the University of Warwick where he chairs the university-wide Graduate School. His main teaching and research interests are in social research methodology, especially qualitative methods, and the sociology of education (particularly the study of schools, classrooms and curricula). He has written ethnographic studies of secondary schools and is currently working on case studies of schools and higher education. His main publications include: *Experiencing Comprehensive Education* (1983), *In the Field: An Introduction to Field Research* (1984), *Education, Schools and Schooling* (1985), *Sociology, Education and Schools* (1986) *Schools at Work* (1988, with Rosemary Deem) *Implementing In-Service Education and Training* (1993, with John Connor, Sheila Galloway, Marlene Morrison and Malcolm Newton) and *Research Methods* (1993), together with fourteen edited volumes on qualitative methods and education. He was recently President of the British Sociological Association and is currently President of the Association for the Teaching of the Social Sciences. He was a member of the ESRC Training Board and is currently a member of the ESRC Research Resources Board.

Helen Connor is an Associate Director at the Institute of Manpower Studies, with overall responsibility for IMS work on education and training issues. She has been involved with research concerning the labour market for highly qualified manpower for over ten years. Publications include: *IT Manpower into the 1990's* (1986), *A Careers Service for Engineering* (1991), *The IMS Graduate Review* (1992), *Evaluation of the Teaching Company Scheme* (1990), *A Review of the Postgraduate Labour Market* (1993). She is currently directing a study for SERC on the demand for PhD scientists, and a European-wide review of the supply and utilisation of scientists and engineers.

Sara Delamont is Reader in Sociology and Director of Graduate Studies in the School of Social and Administrative Studies at the University of Wales, Cardiff. She has published numerous articles and ten books, including *Interaction in the Classroom, Knowledgeable Women* and *Sex Roles and the School*. Her main research areas are the sociology of education (particularly classroom research) and professional socialisation.

David Dunkerley is Professor of Applied Sociology and Dean of Reseach at the University of Plymouth, having previously taught at the Universities of Leeds and Cardiff. Until its demise in 1992, he was Vice-Chair of the Committee for Research at the Council for National Academic Awards. He is presently a member of the Research Grants Board of the Economic and Social Research Council. His main research interests lie in the area of the sociology of organisations and work where he has authored and edited eleven books and numerous articles.

Tim Hill is Co-Director of the ESRC funded research project 'Students, Supervisors and the Social Science Research Training Process'. He previously worked for six years as a primary school teacher and for eleven years as a headteacher of two schools. As Graduate Studies Officer, he was responsible for postgraduate work in the Faculty of Social Sciences at the University of Bristol. He is now responsible for the higher degrees programmes of the School of Education at the University of Bristol where he teaches courses in primary school management and devised the UK's first Doctor of Education Programme.

John Hockey is currently a Research Fellow at Cheltenham and Gloucester College of Higher Education. He was previously a Research Fellow in the Centre for Educational Development, Appraisal and Research at the University of Warwick where he worked on an ESRC funded project examining PhD education in the first year of postgraduate research. Prior to working at CEDAR he taught at Lancashire Polytechnic, Exeter and Lancaster Universities, gaining his PhD at the latter. He has carried out research on nursing morale, mature students' adaptation to University, mental health day care provision, and the military subculture of private soldiers. His research interests include qualitative research methods, socialisation processes and the formation of identities, in particular occupational ones. His publications include the ethnographic study, *Squaddies: Portrait of a Subculture*, and articles in *Studies in Higher Education and Research Papers in Education*.

Aubrey McKennell is Professor Emeritus of Survey Methods at the University of Southampton, and more recently has been director of the RNIB General Needs Survey (HMSO 1992). Early work with the (then) UK Government Social Survey included surveys on the Timing of Holidays, Aircraft Noise Annoyance (leading to the Noise and Number Index) and Smoking Attitudes and Behaviour. He has also published extensively on the perception of quality of life (for example 'Models of Cognition and Affect in Perceptions of Well-being', *Social Indicators Research* (1980), and 'Components of Perceived Life Quality', *Journal of Community Psychology* (1983). He is a specialist in methods of attitude measurement and multivariate analysis of survey data. He has published *Surveying Attitude Structures* (1974) and many journal articles and book chapters on this topic (for example in O'Murcheartaigh and Payne's *The Analysis of Survey Data* (1977). In 1984 he initiated, and remains Coordinator of, the ESRC Survey Link Scheme.

Odette Parry is Lecturer at the University of West Indies. She was a Research Associate in the School of Social and Administrative Studies at the University of Wales, Cardiff. She has had articles recently published in *Sociology*, *Gender and Education* and *Qualitative Studies in Education*. Her main research areas are the sociology of education and professional socialisation.

Estelle Phillips is an Associate Fellow of the British Psychological Society and has served on BPS committees for many years. Her academic posts have included the Tavistock Institute of Human Relations, The London School of Economics, Birkbeck College and The Open University School of Management, where she currently holds a Visiting Research Fellowship. Estelle Phillips also features in several training videos concerned with research and is a regular contributor to radio and television programmes in this country and overseas. Her own PhD thesis is entitled 'The PhD as a Learning Process' and she continues to research this area. She has recently completed an extended tour of Australia, New Zealand and Malaysia where she spoke to research students and academic staff about the skills required in completing and supervising a PhD. She is also a frequent visitor to Universities in Europe. Her main publication is with Derek Pugh *How to Get a PhD* (1987).

Christopher Pole holds a joint post with CEDAR and the Sociology Department at the University of Warwick where he teaches Field Studies in Social Research and Sociology of Education. In CEDAR he is currently engaged in an ESRC funded research project which examines the socialisation and supervision of first year PhD students in the natural sciences. His publications include *Assessing and Recording Achievement: Implementing a New Approach in Schools* (1993), *The Management of TVEI* (1986, with S. Stoney and D. Sims) and *The TVEI Experience*, (1987, with S. Stoney and D. Sims).

Cheryl Schonhardt-Bailey is Lecturer in Government at the London School of Economics and Political Science, and from 1989 to 1991 was a Research Officer. Holding a PhD in Political Science from the University of California, Los Angeles (UCLA), she has published articles in *American Political Science Review*, *World Politics* and *Parliamentary History*, and is currently engaged in research on modelling and quantifying agricultural trade policy, and on theoretical and empirical linkages between national financial systems and interest group formation. Her interests (and current responsibilities) include the teaching of quantitative methods to political scientists, teaching American domestic and foreign economic policy as well as teaching more general courses on political economy.

Glyn Thomas is Senior Lecturer in Psychology at the University of Birmingham. His main research interests are the development of writing skills, the psychology of learning, and drawing and picture perception in children. He has co-authored a text book on children's drawing and has published widely in research journals

Mark Torrance is a Research Fellow in the School of Psychology at the University of Birmingham. He is currently supported by the Leverhulme Trust to work on a longitudinal study of the writing development of undergraduate students. He has published several research articles on the effects of writing strategies.

Jeffrey Weeks is Professor of Social Relations at the University of the West of England, Bristol, and is head of research in the Faculty of Economics and Social Science there. He was formerly an officer responsible for social sciences and research at the Council for National Academic Awards. He is the author of numerous articles and books on various aspects of the social regulation of sexuality, including most recently *Against Nature: Essays on History, Sexuality and Identity* (1991). He is currently working on a book on sexual values, and is co-director (with Peter Aggleton) of an ESRC funded project on *Voluntary Sector Responses to HIV/AIDS*.

Michael Youngman is a Senior Lecturer in Education at the School of Education, University of Nottingham. He has published widely through guide books and articles on aspects of research methodology. He has conducted research on engineering jobs, teaching, nursing and contract research. He is the editor of the *British Journal of Educational Psychology*.

Subject Index

Name Index

Higher Education Policy Series

Graduates at Work
Degree Courses and the Labour Market
John Brennan and Philip McGeevor
ISBN 1 85302 500 3
Higher Education Policy Series 1

Degrees of Success
Career Aspirations and Destinations of College,
University and Polytechnic Graduates
Chris J Boys with John Kirkland
ISBN 1 85302 502 X
Higher Education Policy Series 2

The Use of Performance Indicators in Higher Education
A Critical Analysis of Developing Practice 2nd edition
Martin Cave, Stephen Hanney and Maurice Kogan
ISBN 1 85302 518 6
Higher Education Policy Series 3

Higher Education and the Preparation for Work
*Chris J Boys, John Brennan, Mary Henkel, John Kirkland,
Maurice Kogan and Penny Youll*
ISBN 1 85302 505 4
Higher Education Policy Series 4

Changing Patterns of the Higher Education System
The Experience of Three Decades
*Ulrich Teichler, Universität Gesamthochschule Kassel
Foreword by Eskil Björklund, Secretary,
Research on Higher Education Program, Stockholm, Sweden*
ISBN 1 85302 507 0
Higher Education Policy Series 5

Jessica Kingsley Publishers
116 Pentonville Road, London N1 9JB.

Evaluating Higher Education
Edited by Maurice Kogan
ISBN 1 85302 510 0
Higher Education Policy Series 6

Governmental Strategies and Innovation in Higher Education
Edited by Frans van Vught
ISBN 1 85302 513 5
Higher Education Policy Series 7

Academics and Policy Systems
Edited by Thorsten Nybom and Ulf Lundgren
ISBN 1 85302 512 7
Higher Education Policy Series 8

Major American Higher Education Issues and Challenges in the 1990s
Richard I Miller
ISBN 1 85302 514 3
Higher Education Policy Series 9

Study Abroad Programmes
Edited by B Burn, Ladislav Cerych and Alan Smith
ISBN 1 85302 522 4
Higher Education Policy Series 11, Volume I

Impacts of Study Abroad Programmes on Students and Graduates
Susan Opper, Ulrich Teichler and Jerry Carlson
ISBN 1 85302 523 2
Higher Education Policy Series 11, Volume II

University and Society
Essays on the Social Role of Research and Higher Education
Edited by Martin A. Trow and Thorsten Nybom
ISBN 1 85302 525 9
Higher Education Policy Series 12

Jessica Kingsley Publishers
116 Pentonville Road, London N1 9JB.

Dimensions of Evaluation in Higher Education
Report of the IHME Study Group on Evaluation
in Higher Education
*Urban Dahllöff, John Harris, Michael Shattock, André Staropoli
and Roeland in't Veld*
ISBN 1 85302 526 7
Higher Education Policy Series 13

Learning in Europe
The ERASMUS Experience
A Survey of the 1988-89
ERASMUS Students
Friedhelm Maiworm, Wolfgang Steube and Ulrich Teichler
ISBN 1 85302 527 5
Higher Education Policy Series 14

Self-Regulation in Higher Education
A Multi-National Perspective on Collaborative Systems of
Quality Assurance and Control
H.R. Kells
ISBN 1 85302 528 3
Higher Education Policy Series 15

Higher Education in Europe
Edited by Claudius Gellert
ISBN 1 85302 529 1
Higher Education Policy Series 16

Graduate Education in Britain
Tony Becher, Mary Henkel and Maurice Kogan
ISBN 1 85302 531 3
Higher Education Policy Series 17

Public Expenditure on Higher Education
A Comparative Study in the Member States
of the European Community
*Frans Kaiser, Raymond J.G.M. Florax, Jos. B.J. Koelman,
Frans A. van Vught*
ISBN 1 85302 532 1
Higher Education Policy Series 18

Jessica Kingsley Publishers
116 Pentonville Road, London N1 9JB.

Academic Community
Discourse or Discord?
Edited by Ronald Barnett
ISBN 1 85302 534 8
Higher Education Policy Series 20

Students, Courses and Jobs
The Relationship Between Higher Education and the Labour Market
J L Brennan, E S Lyon, P A McGeevor and K Murray
ISBN 1 85302 538 0
Higher Education Policy Series 21

Innovation and Adaptation in Higher Education
The Changing Conditions of Advanced Teaching and Learning in Europe
Edited by Claudius Gellert
ISBN 1 85302 535 6
Higher Education Policy Series 22

Assessing Quality in Further and Higher Education
Allan Ashworth and Roger Harvey
ISBN 85302 539 9
Higher Education Policy Series 24

Are Professors Professional?
The Organisation of University Examinations
David Warren Piper
ISBN 1 85302 540 2
Higher Education Policy Series 25

Information Technology
Issues for Higher Education Management
Gordon M Bull, Carry Dallinga-Hunter, Yves Epelboin, Edgar Frackmann and Dennis Jennings
ISBN 1 85302 542 9
Higher Education Policy Series 26

Jessica Kingsley Publishers
116 Pentonville Road, London N1 9JB.